Chief Joseph

UNSUNG AMERICANS

CHIEF JOSEPH

Thunder Rolling
Down From The
Mountains

Diana Yates

WARD HILL PRESS

Published by Ward Hill Press
            PO Box 04-0424
            Staten Island, NY 10304-0008
            (718) 816-9449

Excerpts from THE NEZ PERCE INDIANS AND THE OPENING OF THE NORTHWEST by Alvin M. Josephy, Jr. Copyright ©1965 by Alvin M. Josephy, Jr. Reprinted by permission of IMG-Julian Bach Literary Agency, Inc.

Excerpts from HEAR ME, MY CHIEFS! by Lucullus V. McWhorter. Copyright ©1952 by The Caxton Printers. Reprinted by permission.

Excerpts from YELLOW WOLF: HIS OWN STORY by Lucullus V. McWhorter. Copyright ©1991 by The Caxton Printers. Reprinted by permission.

Cover art: Linoleum print by David Adams. Cover design by Jim O'Grady and Diana Yates.

Maps by Diana Yates and Lisa Peet.

Frontispiece: Photo of Chief Joseph, Montana Historical Society, Helena.

Library of Congress Catalog Card No. 92-64127

Publisher's Cataloging in Publication

Yates, Diana, 1962-
     Chief Joseph : thunder rolling down from the mountains / Diana Yates.
     p. cm. -- (Unsung Americans)
     SUMMARY: A biography of Chief Joseph, the Nez Perce chief, and a description of the Nez Perce-American War of 1877.
     ISBN 0-9623380-8-7 (pbk.)
     ISBN 0-9623380-9-5 (library binding)

     1. Joseph, Nez Perce Chief, 1840-1904. 2. Nez Perce Indians--Biography. I. Title. II. Series.

E99.N5Y38 1992   979.5'00497
                                                                    QBI92-1888

For
Mom and George,
Madeline and Jim,
Kaye,
and Jim,
with all my love

Table of Contents

MAPS AND PHOTOGRAPHS

NOTES 134

BIBLIOGRAPHY 135

CHRONOLOGY 136

INDEX 139

Washington

Chief Joseph sat on a platform at the front of the auditorium, staring out at the crowd that had gathered to hear him. This was Washington, D.C., the capital of the white man's world. And this was Lincoln Hall, in the Interior Department building. It was one of the biggest rooms Chief Joseph had ever seen, and it was full of people.

Joseph understood that most of these people were law chiefs: congressmen, cabinet members, diplomats and their wives. And all these men and women had come to hear *his* story. What would he tell them? How would he put into words all that his people had endured?

Finally a white man in a uniform, a war chief named Colonel Meacham, stood up to speak. The room quieted. Joseph's interpreter told him Colonel Meacham would introduce him.

Meacham spoke for a few minutes, then beckoned Joseph forward with a sweep of the hand. The crowd applauded as the chief stepped up, holding his hat in one hand. Chief Joseph stood in the light and waited for the noise to die down.

He was a handsome man, broad-shouldered and tall, with a round face and dark, gentle eyes. His skin was smooth, creased

1

only by the hint of a smile. He wore an embroidered shirt and long pants — clothes a white man might wear. But his hair fell forward in two long braids, and a string of beads gleamed just above his collar. The hair on the top of his head was cut short and swept up into a high forelock, in the style of his people. The hat he held was round and wide-brimmed.

After a few moments the applause faded, and Joseph's interpreter came forward. The chief spoke in his own language. His voice was deep and melodious. He said a few short sentences and then waited patiently while the white man standing next to him translated his words.

"My friends," Joseph began, "I have been asked to show you my heart. I am glad to have a chance to do so. I want the white people to understand my people."

He paused, looking down at his hat.

"Some of you think an Indian is like a wild animal. This is a great mistake. I will tell you all about our people, and then you can judge whether an Indian is a man or not. I believe much trouble and blood would be saved if we opened our hearts more....What I have to say will come from my heart, and I will speak with a straight tongue. The Great Spirit is looking at me, and will hear me."

Beginnings

Chief Joseph looked around the room. He wasn't sure what to say. He wanted his audience to hear the whole story, but how far back did the story go? No one knew how many snows had passed since his people were created. No one knew how many centuries they'd lived before the whites first stumbled across their lands.

"We did not know there were other people besides the Indian until about 100 winters ago, when some men with white faces came to our country," Joseph said. "They brought many things with them to trade for furs and skins.... Our people could not talk with these white-faced men, but they used signs which all people understand. These men were Frenchmen, and they called our people *Nez Perces*" (pierced noses).

When Joseph was a child his grandparents often described their first encounters with the whites, and the stories they told became as real for him as the events of his own life.

"These French trappers said a great many things to our fathers which have been planted in our hearts. Some were good for us, but some were bad. Our people were divided in opinion about these men. Some thought they taught more bad than good....

"An Indian respects a brave man, but he despises a coward. He loves a straight tongue, but he hates a forked tongue. The French trappers told us some truths and some lies."

Joseph glanced at the American flag that stood in the corner of the auditorium. He had seen that flag many times since he was a little boy. As a child he'd found it beautiful. He'd admired its bright colors and perfect lines. But now the sight of it reminded him of the country his people had lost.

Joseph's grandfather was chief when the first American flag was raised over Nez Perce territory. That flag was among the gifts the whites first offered the Nez Perce people.

"The first white men of your people who came to our country were named Lewis and Clark," Joseph said. "They also brought many things that our people had never seen. They talked straight, and our people gave them a great feast, as a proof that their hearts were friendly. These men were very kind. They made presents to our chiefs and our people made presents to them.... All the Nez Perces made friends with Lewis and Clark, and agreed to let them pass through their country....

"It has always been the pride of the Nez Perces that they were friends of the white men....

"My name is Hin-mah-too-yah-lat-kekht" (Thunder Rolling Down From the Mountains), Chief Joseph continued, giving the audience his Indian name. "I am chief of the Wellamotkin band of Chute-pa-lu, or Nez Perces. I was born in eastern Oregon, 38 winters ago."

4

Land of Winding Waters

Joseph's story began in 1840, when he was born in a region the Indians called "Wallowa" (Land of Winding Waters). It was a beautiful country of rolling hills surrounded by mountains and canyons. The land was lush and green and cool, with clear-running rivers and creeks flowing through it like icy veins.

Only Indians lived in the Wallowa country when Joseph was born. Joseph's father, Tuekakas, was chief of the Wallowa band.

Joseph had two older sisters, named Celia and Elawinonmi, and two little brothers, Shugun (Brown) and Ollokot (Frog). All of them stayed with their mother and the other women of the camp. Joseph's mother's name was Khapkhaponimi (Loose Bark on Trees), and she was always busy.

Joseph liked to follow his mother and watch her do her chores. Although she let him and Shugun wander around the camp, Joseph always kept one eye on her whenever they played. It seemed she was always moving around, and he didn't want her to disappear. He was glad she had to carry Ollokot on her back, because the baby slowed her down.

Khapkhaponimi was a strong and handsome woman. She wore a long white buckskin dress, and she kept her hair in two straight braids. Like all Nez Perce women, she had built the family tepee. With an axe she had cut the ridge poles from young pine trees that grew along the river. She had woven mats out of reeds and grasses to form the lodge's waterproof walls. She always kept a fire lit in the middle of the room. Its smoke trailed up through an opening in the "roof" where the ridge poles came together. The lodge was big, but Khapkhaponimi kept it warm inside.

In the early morning hours before sunrise Joseph would sometimes hear her putting wood on the fire. A little later he'd wake up again as she prepared the morning meal. On spring days she took him and his brothers and sisters up the mountainside to dig for roots, and when they returned home she'd spread the roots out in the sun to dry.

Sometimes Joseph went with her into the woods to check the snares, and she showed him how to kill and skin the different animals she caught. He followed her to the lake to gather the reeds that grew along its banks, and he watched while she wove the leaves into the heavy mats that covered the lodge.

When the hunters brought back deer or elk from the hunt, she and the other women set up curing racks over their fires to smoke the meat. And whenever the village moved from one place to another, she pulled down the lodge and packed the horses for the trip.

The Indians often moved their settlements from season to season. In winter they rode down into the canyons on the northern and eastern edges of their land seeking shelter from the heavy snows. In late spring they climbed back up to Wallowa to enjoy the cool breezes of the valley.

They also had to move around to collect different kinds of food. Wild berries ripened on the hillsides each spring, deer and elk came down to the rivers to drink, mountain sheep

The Wallowa Valley, "land of winding waters." (From THE NEZ PERCÉS: TRIBES-MEN OF THE COLUMBIA PLATEAU, by Francis Haines; copyright ©1955 University of Oklahoma Press.)

stalked the highlands, and the rivers churned with salmon fighting their way upstream to spawn. The men often went on hunts for days or weeks to bring in enough meat for their families. The women scoured the hills for roots and berries, and set traps for smaller animals.

For Joseph there was nothing strange about this constant wandering. He looked forward to the spring, when the ice and snow began to melt and the people drove their herds up to the Wallowa Valley to graze. He liked to feel the heat of the sun returning, and watch the older boys fish. He especially loved summer, when there was plenty to eat and when, on hot days, his father took him and his brothers swimming in the lake.

Winter was the most difficult time of year. When the weather was harsh and the wild game scarce, Joseph's mother

A Nez Perce woman poses with her two children. (Special Collections Division, University of Washington Libraries, Negative No. NA 997.)

had to make the leftover fish, nuts, roots and berries last until the spring. The days were cold and empty and the nights were long and dark.

But sometimes in winter Joseph's mother would connect their lodge to the lodges of a few other families, and the people would live together in one long room with many fires. At night the elders would sit around these fires and tell the children the stories of their people. They talked about the clever Coyote and Beaver and all the other animals, and they told how their ancestors were created from the heart of a terrible monster. The elders said it was Beaver who stole the secret of fire from the trees, and they said that long before the people were created the animals got together and decided how long the day and night should be.

Sometimes the elders spoke of great warriors who had lived in earlier days, or of terrible storms that killed many people and left their relatives hungry. They told the children about a time when the buffalo wandered across their lands in herds so big the whole earth rumbled and shook like thunder when they stampeded.

Night after night the elders talked to fill the empty hours. It seemed they knew hundreds of stories about the people who had come before. The elders taught the children their traditions through these stories, and the tales they told about their ancestors also revealed how they wanted their children to live.

"Our fathers gave us many laws, which they had learned from their fathers," Joseph told the men and women in Washington. "They told us to treat all men as they treated us; that we should never be the first to break a bargain; that it was a disgrace to tell a lie; that we should speak only the truth.... We were taught to believe that the Great Spirit sees and hears everything, and that he never forgets.... This I believe, and all my people believe the same."

Learning to Read

When Joseph was a youngster his father often carried him to the Christian mission. The mission was located in a valley called Lapwai (Place of the Butterflies). It took at least two days to get there from Wallowa, but the boy never complained. He loved the ride through the meadows and stands of pine trees and across the rugged Grande Ronde Canyon. He loved crossing the open prairie and the wide Snake River on his father's horse.

Sometimes his father would spot animal tracks in a meadow, or in the mud of a riverbank, and he'd show Joseph how to read these prints to see how old they were. A fresh piece of broken grass meant that the tracks were also fresh. A dried-out footprint in the mud meant the animal was already far away.

At the mission school the white woman showed the boy another kind of tracks. These were the little scratches on paper his father said were the marks of different words. The missionary would point to a mark, and then tell Joseph what it said. But Joseph found it easier to read the prints of a deer or a raccoon.

The white woman had already taught Joseph's father how to read. Her husband had given the chief a copy of their Book of Heaven, which they called the Bible. It was a treasure he

Nez Perce rider. (Special Collections Division, University of Washington Libraries, Negative No. NA 1009.)

carried with pride. Sometimes at night in the lodge Joseph saw his father whispering to this sacred book, and apparently the book whispered back because he told Joseph what it said.

It wasn't long before other whites came to Nez Perce territory. Soon caravans of immigrants began appearing in the south. Sometimes Joseph saw their travel-worn wagons crawling west across the Grande Ronde Valley.

Each year the wagon trains got longer, and their ragged trails widened into roads. Hundreds of wagons snaked through the valley, like a river of horses and carts and cows. Most of the immigrants moved on. But each year more arrived.

Some of the Indians resented these invasions of their country. At night around the fires of the council meetings the medicine men shook their fists. Soon, they warned their people, the white men and women would come to stay.

These dark predictions worried Joseph, who was still only a child. But the medicine men were not the only ones who warned their people about the newcomers. Warriors returned from the buffalo country with frightening stories they'd heard on the trail. In the east, the travelers said, whole tribes had been scattered, moved or slaughtered by whites who then took over their lands.

The warriors' stories troubled Joseph, but they were hard to understand. He could not imagine the whites he saw in the wagon trains pushing his people off their lands. Only a few of those who came west had even stopped to settle in the area. They were just families looking for homes; surely they were no threat to the Indian people.

By the time the first snows came the wagon trains disappeared. Joseph knew it would take another nine months for the next flood of newcomers to arrive. Snow buried the travelers' roads, hiding the evidence of their crossing. But in the spring when the snow melted, the marks of their wagon wheels reappeared. These trails were another set of tracks young Joseph would need to learn to read.

Inheritance

Many years later, in the summer of 1871, Tuekakas sent for Joseph and Joseph's younger brother, Ollokot. The old chief's camp lay deep in the Wallowa country, and when Joseph got to him he saw that his father was dying.

For a few years Tuekakas had been losing his sight. At first he got around with the help of a boy who guided his horse. But he had become feeble and could no longer manage as he once had. Joseph had already taken his place as chief of the Wallowa band. Joseph was 31 years old.

That day, as his father's concentration faded, Joseph held his hand and quietly reviewed what he remembered of his life. Tuekakas was now in his 80s and, for the most part, his life had been happy. But Joseph could see the pain of the last few years carved in his father's face.

In that time Tuekakas had seen the white people swarm across the country. He'd watched them establish their settlements and ranches as if the land belonged to them. He did not protest when the Americans brought in their soldiers and built their forts, and he remained quiet when the settlers raised fences, plowed fields and began to graze their cattle on the open land.

He said nothing when they divided Nez Perce territory between three states, for the names Washington, Idaho and Oregon made little difference to him. And when the Americans asked the Indians to live on a reservation, Tuekakas signed their treaty because the reservation included his lands.

But he would not accept the gifts and money the Americans offered him. He said there was no reason to take their payments, for he had given nothing away.

It was not long before Tuekakas discovered that the reservation boundaries were meaningless. His signature on the treaty paper could not keep the white people out. White ranchers drove their cattle onto the rich grasslands of the lower country. White prospectors crossed onto Nez Perce lands, panning the rivers for bits of gold. So many whites moved into Nez Perce territory that the government officials returned, asking the Indians for more land and talking about a new reservation. This one would be in the state the whites called Idaho. It was a tiny piece of country, compared to the wide territory the Nez Perces already held.

Tuekakas and several other chiefs walked out of this meeting with the Americans. They saw no reason to sign a treaty that stripped them of the lands they loved. But the government officials had come for signatures, and they refused to leave empty-handed. With extravagant promises they convinced the other chiefs to sign the treaty papers, and they claimed that all the Nez Perce Indians were bound by the new agreement.

In his father's lodge that day Joseph sat and watched the old man sleep. Tuekakas had suffered many losses over the years. There had been wars between the Americans and the neighboring Indian tribes, wars that left the Indians homeless and the whites a little richer. Tuekakas had only narrowly avoided joining his neighbors in these battles, and he grieved for the innocent Indians killed when the soldiers stormed across their lands. His wife had died, and his middle son, Shugun, had been murdered in an argument with another Nez Perce Indian. The death of his son had crushed Tuekakas. Almost three years had passed since then, but the old chief had never completely recovered.

Tuekakas stirred. For a moment his sightless eyes searched the emptiness, and then, remembering, he closed them again. Joseph squeezed his hand reassuringly.

"My son," the old man began to speak, and Joseph leaned close to hear every word. "My body is returning to my mother earth, and my spirit is going very soon to see the Great Spirit Chief." His voice was frail at first but as he continued it got stronger. "When I am gone, think of your country. You are the chief of these people. They look to you to guide them. Always remember your father never sold his country."

The old man's eyes fluttered for a moment as he paused to catch his breath. His love of his country was the one thing that had kept him going the last few years. After the second treaty, he had put up a line of poles to guard the entrance to the Wallowa. He wanted to show the whites that the land belonged to his people.

"You must stop your ears whenever you are asked to sign a treaty selling your home," Tuekakas continued. "A few years more, and white men will be all around you. They have their eyes on this land....

"My son, never forget my dying words. This country holds your father's body. Never sell the bones of your father and your mother."

"I pressed my father's hand and told him I would protect his grave with my life," Joseph remembered. "My father smiled and passed away to the spirit-land."

Joseph buried his father's body at the base of a hill above his camp, and the Indians raised a circle of poles around his grave to mark the spot. They slaughtered one of his horses and hung its carcass over the burial site. The chief would need his horse to carry him to the good land. Above the horse's body they suspended a bell on a red pole. The bell, a symbol of the momentous importance of the headman's death, rang whenever the wind swept over his grave.

"I buried him in that beautiful land of winding waters," Joseph said. "I love that land more than all the rest of the world."

Like Deer
and Grizzly Bears

The same year Tuekakas died, the first white settlers pushed into the Wallowa country looking for homes. Before, they had only settled in the lower Nez Perce territory, unwilling to brave the steep mountains and canyons that surrounded the Wallowa lands. But in 1871 they came up out of the Grande Ronde Valley and moved across the western mountains, and they drove their horses and cattle through the line of poles Tuekakas had raised.

When Joseph told these newcomers they were trespassing in Indian territory, they said that, as far as they knew, the American government had bought the Wallowa lands.

Chief Joseph patiently explained that his people had never sold the Wallowa. They'd never signed a treaty giving the white people rights to their lands, nor had they taken any money from the government. This territory had always belonged to them, he said, and they would not sell it at any price.

But the settlers said their land claims had been authorized by the government. If there was a problem, they told Joseph, it was up to the government to solve it. In the meantime, they said, they would build their cabins and graze their horses and cattle on the lush grasslands of the Wallowa Valley.

Chief Joseph was disappointed, but he continued to visit the settlers. And although he was frustrated by their stubbornness, he always treated them with respect. Sometimes he sat with a family for hours, politely discussing other matters. Sometimes he played with their children, amusing them with games his own children enjoyed.

He was a striking figure — a tall and handsome man who moved and talked with quiet dignity. He rarely smiled, but he was usually gentle and considerate. Joseph's serious manner impressed the whites, and his ability to listen made them more willing to negotiate. Soon a few of the settlers decided to visit the reservation agent, to ask who actually owned the Wallowa.

When the agent, a man named John Monteith, heard there was trouble in the valley, he hurried out to meet with Joseph and the other Indians. Monteith hoped to convince them to give up the Wallowa. He too believed that the Wallowa Indians had sold their lands to the government. But Joseph again explained that this father had never signed the second treaty.

Like the settlers, the agent was impressed by Joseph's manner. He, too, had some questions about the treaty. But for the moment he was powerless to do much, so he urged the Indians and the whites to try to share the Wallowa country. He told Joseph the whites would need only a little land. When he heard this, the chief agreed to let the settlers stay.

The Indians spent that winter in the canyons as they always did, but when they returned to Wallowa more newcomers had settled in the valley. The Indians' grazing ranges were now occupied by the settlers' herds. A number of cabins dotted the hillsides, and a few fences zigzagged across the land.

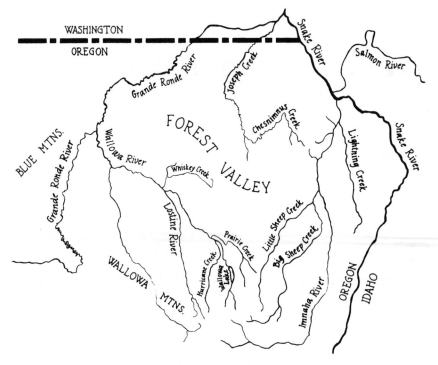

The Wallowa country.

Chief Joseph looked out across the valley without understanding the changes he saw. Somehow his home had become an unfamiliar place. A strange people had taken over his father's country, and the laws his parents and grandparents lived by no longer applied in this new world.

Joseph knew his own people would look to him for guidance, but he felt helpless. How could he stop the white people from taking over his country? How could a little group of Indians hold back a human flood?

"We were like deer. They were like grizzly bears," Joseph explained. "We had a small country. Their country was large. We were contented to let things remain as the Great Spirit Chief made them. They were not, and would change the rivers and the mountains if they did not suit them."

The President's Pledge

Two years later John Monteith told Chief Joseph that the "great father" in Washington had approved a Wallowa reservation. President Ulysses S. Grant would allow the Indians to keep the northern part of the Wallowa. He was giving the rest of the Wallowa territory to the whites.

Although Joseph was confused by the strange division of his country, he agreed to this arrangement. He would do whatever he could to keep his people in the Wallowa. He was happy that at least the American government had recognized his land claims. For the first time in years, his people's future seemed secure.

But the white settlers were outraged by the president's decision. They refused to leave the northern part of the Wallowa to the Indians. They said they would not give up their homes to a bunch of unruly Indians, and although the government promised to pay them for their property, some insisted they would never leave.

The whites continued to graze their horses and cattle on both sides of the president's reservation line and, as the weeks slid by, conditions in the Wallowa worsened. The Indians and the whites watered their animals at the same creeks and springs.

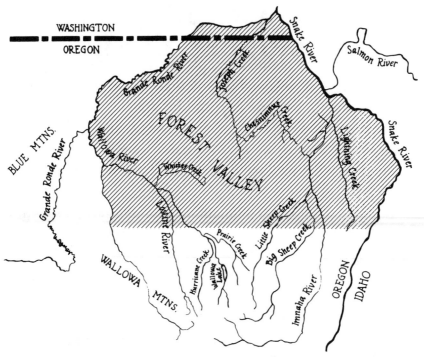

Proposed Wallowa reservation.

Sometimes their herds got mixed together, and heated arguments erupted when the ranchers and warriors tried to separate the animals.

Sometimes the young men of Joseph's band talked of revenge. They said the Indians should get together and drive the whites out of the valley. Their resentment grew stronger every time there was a problem, and Joseph and the other headmen found it difficult to restrain them.

That winter more settlers moved into the reservation area and, as warm weather approached, the tension between the whites and Indians grew. In the summer of 1874, a few white men seized some grazing ranges and threatened to shoot any Indians that came near. Although other, more level-headed settlers eventually convinced these men to withdraw, the harm was already done. The fierce competition for land now ruined all Chief Joseph's efforts for peace.

A few settlers blamed Joseph for the problems in the Wallowa. They called him a troublemaker, and they did whatever they could to provoke him and his men.

"They stole a great many horses from us, and we could not get them back because we were Indians," Joseph recalled. "The white men told lies for each other. They drove off a great many of our cattle."

But when Joseph complained to the agent, Monteith blamed the *Indians* for the troubles, and he told Joseph he should move his people to the *Idaho* reservation.

Joseph was bewildered. What about the president's pledge? Hadn't Monteith just told him his people now held a reservation in the Wallowa? Who would protect the reservation, he wondered, if not the officials who had created it? Were the whites not bound by any laws, even those put forth by their own leaders?

In 1875, Joseph finally got his answer. That summer John Monteith sent word for him to come to Lapwai. Joseph and a few of his men made the trip to the agent's office, and when they got there Monteith told them the president had changed his mind about the Wallowa reservation. Monteith told Joseph there was nothing he could do. He said it would be best if Joseph moved his people to Idaho as soon as possible.

Joseph was furious. He argued with Monteith, declaring that the Wallowa belonged to the Indians. But the agent ignored Joseph's claims, and said the Indians had sold their lands. In a rage, Joseph stormed out of Monteith's office. Without another word to the agent, he and his men rode out of Lapwai.

The Wheel

Summer was in full flower, the river was calm, and cool breezes swept across the land, making the prairie grasses shimmer like silky fur. As Joseph and his companions rode across the prairie, grasshoppers bounded out of the grass in front of their horses, bees zigzagged, and black flies landed on the horses' necks, making them twitch with irritation. The land bristled with life.

But as they headed home the horsemen were silent, burdened by the grim news they carried. Joseph dreaded having to look into his people's expectant faces. How could he explain the American government's reversal? How could he tell them the president had changed his mind?

When they reached the dark woods beyond the prairie Joseph stopped to look back across the open land. He could not say how many times he had made this journey to Lapwai and back. He had been carried there as an infant, then as a boy on his father's horse, then as a young man he had guided his own horse. Now he made the trip as chief of the Wallowa people.

He had spent his whole life traveling back and forth between the Indian and the white worlds, and each time he made the trip it seemed the distance from one to the other changed.

It felt like the earth was shrinking, as if the whites were swallowing the land they claimed. They cut the earth with fences, they divided it with roads, and they covered its surface with fields. Soon there would be nothing but farms and roads, trading posts, mills, houses and schools and churches stretching out to the horizon where now there was only this high plain of silky grass.

As he looked back over the prairie, Joseph realized he had waited too long to protect his lands. White civilization was like a giant wheel that rolled faster and faster until nothing could stop it. It was a wagon wheel that crushed all the obstacles in its path.

It would have been easier to resist it at the beginning. Now too many homes had been built, too many fields plowed, too many horses and cattle brought in.

Joseph guided his horse into the shadowy dampness of the pine forest, his mind a jumble of painful memories and dark thoughts. He had believed the government's promise. He had imagined that the great wheel would also carry his people forward, like the whites, into a safe and prosperous future. At last, it seemed, the whites had recognized that the Indians were people, and that they had the same needs for light and air and space and liberty.

But he had been deceived. Now he saw that the great wheel was not meant for Indians. To the wheel the Indian people were just so many stones littering the road. Red stones in the path of progress. Some were small enough to be ridden over; others had to be removed.

Year after year the specter of war had haunted the Nez Perce people. It was a trickster with many faces: it was a beautiful woman that beckoned to the young warriors with whispered promises of glory; it was a demon that lashed out at them with insults. It infuriated the people and then it offered them consolation. Sometimes it was their greatest torment, sometimes it seemed their only hope.

For years Joseph's people had resisted the call to violence. In council after council the headmen agreed it would be foolish to fight the Americans. None of them wanted to add their tribe to the long list that had already been shattered by the whites.

Chief Joseph avoided the settlers, gave up important pastures, and tolerated the occasional presence of troops on his people's lands. He restrained his young warriors in moments of crisis, but he could see that their resistance was wearing away. As one by one their hopes were destroyed, the trickster's power over them increased.

War was coming. Not even Joseph could stop it.

Friends

Chance first brought Chief Joseph face to face with General Oliver Otis Howard, the man who would one day drive him and his people from their lands. In early 1875, Joseph was visiting relatives at the Umatilla Reservation when he heard that an important government official was there. Joseph was still waiting for word on the Wallowa reservation, so he asked to speak with Howard. It was a meeting he would never forget.

Joseph had stepped forward to grasp General Howard's hand. Before letting go, the Wallowa chief gazed into his eyes for a few moments.

The white man had a kind face, but his eyes were deep-set and sad. He had bushy eyebrows and a thick beard that came to a point just below his chin. His nose was long and wide, and his lower lip protruded slightly, which gave him a determined look. He was in uniform, with stars on his shoulders like those Joseph had seen on the American flag, and glimmering buttons down his chest and an enormous, shining belt. His right sleeve was pinned up. Joseph realized he must have lost his arm in battle. The Wallowa chief was impressed.

"I heard that Washington had some message for me," Joseph began, but the general looked at him blankly.

"There is no word from Washington," Howard said, but when he saw the look of disappointment on Joseph's face, he quickly added, "we are glad to see you and shake you by the hand," and the meeting ended abruptly.

This brief encounter with Joseph made an impression on the general. The solemn handshake and the chief's quiet respectfulness surprised and pleased Howard. "I think Joseph and I became then quite good friends," the general later wrote.

General Howard had authority over a vast territory in the northwest United States, which included all the Nez Perce Indian lands. He was in a position to help Chief Joseph and the other Indians. But in the years ahead, he would turn out to be anything but the Indians' friend.

A few months after his meeting with Joseph, Howard asked his assistant, Major Henry Clay Wood, to study the Nez Perce treaties to see if the Wallowa Indians had really sold their lands. In January 1876, Wood came back with his answer. He told the general the second treaty did not apply to Joseph's band; the Wallowa Indians had never sold their lands.

But Howard didn't tell the agent, John Monteith, about these findings. Nor did he notify the settlers that they were trespassing on Indian lands.

Instead, Howard arranged a council meeting with the Indians. He was a military man, with thousands of soldiers ready to follow his commands. There were only a few hundred Nez Perces living in the disputed territory. The general was confident that, under the circumstances, he would be able to convince the chief to move his people to Idaho.

Power Is Not Justice

Joseph's council meeting with General Howard had begun. Joseph sat in the mission church, in a pew at the front of the sanctuary. A dismal light leaked through the windows. The treaty commissioners were making their opening speeches.

The room was packed with Indians: Joseph's men and a few others on the left, with men from the reservation filling the right and center sections. The Indians sat and listened without moving or responding.

Joseph coldly surveyed the row of commissioners perched in chairs at the front of the room. There was General Howard. And there was Major Wood, whom he had trusted. The other men he did not know and it didn't matter. They all spoke with one voice anyway, one intent.

When the white men spoke, they stacked their lies one upon another, the way the Indians stacked stones in the swollen rivers each spring to trap the struggling fish. Joseph's people were the fish the commissioners hoped to snare with their barriers made of words. But the white men spoke too quickly, each sentence thrown down upon the last, as if they knew the structure of their arguments would not hold. Joseph listened calmly as they recited all the familiar declarations.

The Indians were bound by the second treaty, the commissioners said, and must now give up the Wallowa lands. After all, they continued, the Nez Perce people had made a trade and were required to stick by it. Besides, the commissioners said, the land now belonged to the state of Oregon and because of this the president could not return it to the Indians even if he wanted to. They said the Indians could not be protected from the whites. They said the valley had already been opened for settlement. They said more settlers would come. They said the area was too cold for Indians. Joseph raised an eyebrow at this — too cold? Now that was an interesting argument.

The commissioners ended by promising that the government would "in a spirit of generosity...treat for an adjustment of present difficulties." In other words, although the American government did not recognize the Nez Perces' claim to the Wallowa country, they would pay Joseph's people to leave it.

Finally the commissioners finished and it was Joseph's turn to speak. After a long moment he stood up. He would, he'd decided, try again to help them see that the Indians could not be separated from their lands. He would explain that to ask the Indians to give up their land was like asking them to give up their parents. Joseph's father and mother were buried in that valley. All the Indian people who had come before had been buried there and were now part of the earth.

My son, my body is returning to mother earth, his father had said. *Never sell the bones of your father and your mother.* His people could not consent to live as orphans. How could he, as their chief, agree to such a thing? It was impossible.

Joseph looked steadily at the commissioners as he spoke. "The Creating Power," he began, "when he made the earth, made no marks, no lines of division or separation on it. The earth is my mother. I was made of the earth and grew up on its bosom. The earth, as my mother and nurse, is very sacred to me; too sacred to be valued or sold for gold or silver. I cannot give up my mother, the land that raised me.... I ask nothing of the president. I am able to take care of myself."

Joseph waited as the interpreter repeated his statement. The commissioners sat in silence, unimpressed by his heartfelt words. Finally one of them responded: "The president is not interested in taking away your rights," he said, "he wants only to subject you to the same just and equal laws to which he and all his people are subjected."

A few of Joseph's men shifted uneasily in their seats but Joseph remained standing. He closed his eyes for a long moment.

How could the commissioner tell him that the president wanted to treat the Indians the same as whites? Would a white man be compelled to sell his property against his will? Would a white man be forced from his home, stripped of his freedom and religion and penned like an animal on a reservation? Would a white man's murder go unpunished?

Joseph thought of Wilhautyah, a young warrior from his band who'd been wrongly accused of stealing a white man's horses? When Wilhautyah denied the charge, one of his accusers attacked him. When he defended himself, another white man shot and killed him. Wilhautyah's white murderers had never been punished for their crime.

Just outside the windows at the back of the church, Wilhautyah's grieving wife and daughter waited with the other women of the camp. What would they say if they could hear the commissioners' words? What did the white man's law mean to them?

Joseph had seen how some Indians had accepted the white men's promises, adapted to their ways, and lost themselves. Seated in the church that day was Reuben, Joseph's own brother-in-law, the head chief of the Indians who had signed the treaties. Once called Tipyahlanah Oikelazikin, Reuben had been transformed over the years. He had grown rich in the days of the gold rush. When white prospectors first appeared on Indian lands he had helped them in every way, going so far as to build a warehouse and a ferry for the miners well inside the reservation boundaries. Within only a few months the young headman had adopted the clothes and habits of a white man. He lived in a log house, not far from his prosperous ferry. He had become a farmer, a rancher, a property owner.

Now Reuben looked at Joseph anxiously and Joseph wondered what he wanted him to say. Joseph glanced at the faces of the other reservation Indians. Most sat with their eyes fixed on the commissioners. Others stared back blankly, their expressions impossible to read. Were they angry? Were they indifferent? Joseph wondered. Even though the Americans had not fulfilled any of the promises they'd made, even though these Indians had been cheated, they were afraid to challenge the whites. They had become a frightened, docile people.

And now the government wanted Joseph's people to share their cage? No, the chief repeated, his people would not be needing the reservation.

One of the commissioners threw his hands up in frustration. "What shall we say to the president when we get back?" he almost shouted.

"All I have to say is that I love my country," Joseph replied.

"Suppose several thousand men should come from Oregon with arms," General Howard asked. "What would you

Joseph looked at the white man steadily, fully aware that his people were being threatened. "We will not sell the land," he said quietly, surprised by his own sudden resolve. "We will not give up the land. We love the land. It is our home."

And with that Joseph sat down. The chief had nothing more to say.

When the Indians had gone the commissioners put together a report for Washington, proposing that Joseph's people be given a deadline for removal to the reservation. If the Indians refused to leave the Wallowa, the report recommended that they "should then be placed by force upon the Nez Perce reservation."

Everyone signed this report except Major Wood. Although Wood believed the Indians would have to go onto the reservation eventually, he was opposed to the idea of initiating any military action against them.

"I recognize that the Indian must yield to the white man," he wrote in his own report, "but power is not justice, force is not law."

It took little more than a month for the Commissioner of Indian Affairs in Washington, D.C., to approve the recommendation of the majority. One way or another, it had been decided, the Indians *would* go on the Nez Perce reservation. As Howard put it, "the time for loving persuasion had now gone by. Positive *instructions* had come, and *obedience* was required."

Obedience

There would be only one more winter for Joseph's people in the canyons they called home. This would be the last season of peace they would know. Their time in the mountains of northeastern Oregon was coming to an end.

On their way to the Imnaha Canyon they walked the trails their ancestors had followed, ancient trails with no known origin. Centuries of travel had cut into the powdery soil: processions of women and men and children and dogs carrying their villages on their backs, and later the biting hooves of horses and gigantic herds of cattle. This was the last time they would make this journey. Soon the trails would begin to fade, masked by neglect and dust.

When they had selected a campsite the women rebuilt their village not far from the Imnaha River, digging out the floors of their lodges as they had always done, and piling the earth up around their homes to guard against the winter chill. They put their lodges close to one another, seeking added security and comfort in the shelter of the village.

Chief Joseph watched as his people prepared for winter. Here, at least for a few months, they would be safe, removed from the troubles that plagued them up in the Wallowa country.

Winter was a gift. As a boy Joseph had dreaded it. Now he welcomed it. This camp was no different from the winter camps of his childhood. Here was the quiet routine, the settling in. Here the beauty of the land survived in canyons still unwanted and untouched by the white settlers. Here was the harmony, here was the peace Joseph longed for.

But even this haven would be invaded, this precious quiet interrupted. In late January 1877, four reservation Indians found Joseph's camp in the canyon and asked to speak with the chief. The visitors said they had a message from Lapwai.

They said that Monteith wanted the Wallowa Indians to move onto the reservation by April 1st. They said Monteith had set this deadline with the government's approval and Joseph would do well to meet it. The reservation Indians warned Joseph that it would be dangerous to refuse.

Joseph was alarmed by the Indians' message but would not yield to their demands. Monteith's vague threats only angered the Wallowa chief.

"I have been talking to the whites many years about the land in question," he told his visitors, "and it is strange they cannot understand me. The country they claim belonged to my father, and when he died it was given to me and my people, and I will not leave it until I am compelled to."

Unable to convince Joseph to change his mind, the visitors mounted their horses and set out again for Lapwai, shaking their heads in dismay. Joseph was relieved to see them go.

But their visit upset the Wallowa people. No one knew what the ultimatum meant. If they did not meet the deadline, would the whites think they wanted to go to war?

Soon Joseph was troubled by doubts. *I will not leave until compelled to,* he had said. Had he given Monteith the wrong

Chief Joseph's winter camp. (Special Collections Division, University of Washington Libraries, Negative No. NA 940.)

impression? If so, the misunderstanding would have to be corrected. So Joseph decided to send to Lapwai a messenger he could trust. He summoned Ollokot, his brother.

Ollokot was younger than Joseph and as different as a brother could be. While Joseph was measured, solemn and careful, Ollokot was boisterous and daring. A courageous hunter and warrior, Ollokot was revered as a war chief. Joseph always consulted him in difficult moments. Although he was impetuous and an aggressive warrior, Ollokot always deferred to his brother. Having earned the respect of the young warriors, he was best able to restrain them. He had become indispensable to Joseph. He was his closest advisor and companion, and in the grueling months ahead the two would rarely be seen apart.

Ollokot made two trips to Lapwai, meeting first with Monteith and then with Howard. Joseph also sent him to the Umatilla Reservation for an interview with the agent there.

Although Ollokot assured the government men that his people did not want to fight, little else was accomplished. When he met with Howard, Ollokot said his people might be willing to live on the *Umatilla* reservation, but Howard rejected the idea. Then Ollokot proposed that a new reservation be created in the Wallowa and Imnaha country. He said the Wallowas and the Indians from the Umatilla reservation could live there, giving up the current Umatilla reservation lands. Again Howard said no. He would consider no new proposals, he told the young warrior, because, as he put it, "the instructions are definite."

Later Howard would claim he was following the instructions of his superiors. This made it easier for him to deny responsibility for the disastrous consequences of his policy to force the Wallowas onto the Idaho reservation. But it was his policy, and his alone. He had written it; his superiors had only given their approval. Surely he could have altered the plan to avoid the expense and hardship of war.

Officials in the War Department were very nervous about the possibility of war with the Indians. Only a year before, a Sioux chief called Sitting Bull had escaped American forces by retreating across the Montana border into Canada. There had been a public outcry against the war with the Sioux, and the Secretary of War was anxious to avoid any other conflicts.

But Howard would not compromise with the Indians. Instead he chose to demand obedience. He did not consider Joseph and Ollokot his equals. Instead he spoke to them (and about them) as if they were lazy and obstinate children who needed a spanking. Like most white men of his time, Howard

36

General O.O. Howard.
(Library of Congress.)

considered Indians inferior to whites. "Smart as these youths were," he wrote of Joseph and Ollokot, "their tendency to evil...was undoubtedly inherited."

In the end another council was scheduled at Lapwai. This time all the Indians of the region would be invited to attend, except for those already on the reservation. The date was set for early May. Ollokot took his leave of General Howard and hurried back to Joseph with the news.

"Really matters did not look much like war," Howard later wrote.

The Last Council

The snow was melting. It lay in heaps in the lower passes and turned to slush. The trail dipped in and out of these drifts and sometimes disappeared altogether. The horses made slow progress.

Up higher the ground was clear but the horses tripped and slid on the slippery trail. In most places the earth was still cool and wet and muddy, soaked with spring rains and melt. Tiny streams trickled between the rocks and hillocks and collected in hollows along the slopes. Small pools filled up and spilled over again and formed new streams. They washed along the hillsides carrying small rocks and sediment and cutting crooked channels in the earth until at last they found the river.

The Snake River had swollen with floodwater. The Wallowas had to struggle to cross it, and even as they rode away, the river's thunder followed them for a while. Joseph looked back at it. This was no time to travel. In a few weeks, this river would be almost impossible to cross.

Finally the hills of Lapwai came into view. With Joseph and Ollokot in the lead, the Indians streamed into the valley.

Howard and the other whites who waited at the post were startled when they saw the line of Indians moving slowly through the hills. Even from a distance this procession looked strange — as if they marched in a silent parade. As the Indians drew nearer the whites could see their painted faces and colorful clothes. The men wore elaborate buckskin leggings and shirts, some trimmed with fur and painted with patterns. They wore their hair in perfect braids "tied up with showy strings." Some sported hats like those the white men wore.

The women wrapped up in bright shawls or blankets and wore long skirts and beaded moccasins. Each rider was decorated. Some wore garments studded with beads, others arrayed themselves with feathers or ribbons that captured the light and fluttered in the breeze. All sat on horses as various in color as their clothes.

When they reached the high fence that surrounded the fort, the Indians cupped their hands over their mouths and began to sing. The sounds they made were like nothing the whites had ever heard. The song, Howard later recalled, "was shrill and searching; sad, like a wail, and yet defiant."

Still singing, the Indians marched along the outside of the fence. Instead of entering when they reached the gate, they passed it by. The whites inside the fence watched the Indians nervously, not knowing what to expect. Three times the Indians circled the compound, all the while chanting their song.

One woman asked Howard if he thought the Indians wanted to fight. Howard said no. "Yet somehow," the general later admitted, "this wild sound produced a strange effect. It made one feel glad that there were 50 of them, and not 500."

Only the reservation Indians understood the importance of this parade. This ceremony had been repeated whenever the Nez Perces met an enemy in council. The solemn procession expressed their determination, their faith in themselves, their

power. They wanted to remind the whites that they were a power to be respected.

Finally the Indians stacked their weapons outside the gate and filed inside. Joseph, Ollokot and a chief from the Umatilla Reservation led Joseph's men to the meeting place. A large, open-sided tent had been set up for the occasion. Inside the tent Howard waited with his aides. John Monteith was also there. James Reuben and a white man named Perrin Whitman stood to one side. Reuben and Whitman were to act as interpreters during the council. Joseph noticed a few soldiers standing around as well.

Besides the chiefs and a few prominent men from Joseph's camp, there were no other Indians in the tent. The rest of Joseph's people gathered outside. Several reservation Indians huddled at the edge. Apparently the Wallowas were the first band to arrive for the council.

Prewar Nez Perce dreamers. (Historical Photograph Collections, Washington State University Libraries, Negative No. 82-026.)

Howard was anxious to begin. But Joseph wanted the council postponed until all the other Indians from the region arrived. He did not want to speak for those he did not represent.

But Howard would not be delayed. "Mr. Monteith's instructions and mine are directly to YOUR people," he told Joseph.

Two old men of Joseph's camp stood up, their creased faces drawn into expressions of concern. "On account of coming generations, the children and the children's children, of both whites and Indians," the first one said, motioning toward Perrin Whitman, "you must interpret correctly." And then the other promptly added, "We want to talk a long time, many days, about the earth, about our land."

Howard nodded impatiently. "I will listen to all you say," he said to the two, "but you might as well know at the outset that in every extent the Indians must obey the orders of the government of the United States."

A sudden breeze swept through the valley, driving a cloud of dust across the ground. The roof of the council tent swelled and lifted, and then exhaled, for a few long moments its fluttering the only sound. The Indians were silent, astonished at the hostile manner of the one they called Cut-Off Arm. *The Indians must obey,* he'd said. What kind of talk was this? He spoke like a haughty Blackleg, or a Sioux caught up in battle. No Indian who wished for peace would talk like this *in council.*

The Indians said nothing so Monteith stood up. He held a paper with words from Washington on it: his "instructions." When he finished reading, Monteith glared at the Indians.

"I sent out Reuben and some others to your camp, and invited you to come in," he muttered gruffly. "Now you must come, and there is no getting out of it.... General Howard will stay till matters are settled."

General Howard will stay. And what was meant by that? The thought of General Howard staying was not supposed to give the Indians comfort. No, when Monteith said "General Howard," it was General Howard's army he imagined. With General Howard's army at his back, Monteith had become a courageous man.

Another difficult moment passed in silence. Finally Ollokot got to his feet. He looked composed but his voice wavered with emotion. "We have respect for the whites," he said loudly, "but they treat me as a dog, and I sometimes think my friends are different from what I had supposed. There should be *one law* for all."

Howard replied deliberately and slowly. "Agent Monteith and myself are under the same government," he said, carefully pronouncing each word as if he spoke to simpletons. "What it commands us to do, that we must do.... If the Indians hesitate

*Ollokot, Joseph's brother.
(From THE NEZ PERCÉS:
TRIBESMEN OF THE
COLUMBIA PLATEAU,
by Francis Haines.
Copyright ©1955,
Univ. of Oklahoma Press.)*

to come to the reservation, the government directs that soldiers be used to bring them hither."

Here it was, the naked threat. The general was "showing them the rifle," as the Indians described it. The Indians must obey. If they refused, it would mean war.

The meeting began to fall apart. The Indians insisted that they must wait for the other participants before the council could continue. But Howard would not let up, and threatened those who spoke against him, saying he would arrest them and send them to the Indian Territory if they persisted. This statement had a quieting effect; immediately the frightened Indians backed down.

Once the Indians had "changed their tone," the general agreed to postpone the council until the other bands arrived.

He was confident he could badger them all into submission.

When dealing with obstinate Indians, Howard would later advise, "fearless sternness always produced the most wholesome and immediate consequences."

On the second day, Joseph announced that the Indians had chosen a speaker to represent them all in council, an old Snake River Indian named Toohoolhoolzote. Several bands of Indians had finally straggled in, and the crowd in and around the council tent had swelled.

Toohoolhoolzote was a spirited opponent and a zealous defender of his people's rights. Although an old man, he was large and muscular and spoke with a deep and husky voice. When he stood up to speak, the white men eyed him nervously.

"I have heard about a bargain, a trade between some of these Indians and the white men concerning their land," the old man said, "but I belong to the land out of which I came. The earth is my mother."

"The Nez Perces did make such an agreement," Howard replied, and he said that all the Indians must honor the pledge some of the chiefs had made at the signing of the second treaty.

"The government at Washington cannot think for us," Toohoolhoolzote said fiercely.

Howard was alarmed by the Indian's boldness. The old man's words inspired the other Indians. Howard could see them exchanging looks of satisfaction as he spoke.

When Toohoolhoolzote finished speaking, Joseph asked that the council be delayed. Howard readily agreed, even suggesting that the discussion be postponed until the following Monday, keeping Saturday and Sunday free. He would need time to bring the soldiers in.

Over the weekend he sent for several detachments of men, ordering them to guard against a possible attack. These soldiers could also force the Wallowas off their lands if they refused to follow his orders.

That weekend more Indians arrived for the council. On Sunday some reservation Indians reported that the bands were meeting and singing war songs.

The council began again on Monday morning, and Toohoolhoolzote took up where he had left off three days before. He was "crosser and more impudent in his abruptness of manner than before," Howard complained.

Howard decided to interrupt the speaker. "We do not wish to interfere with your religion," he suddenly snarled, "but you must talk of practicable things. Twenty times over you repeat that the earth is your mother, and about chieftainship from the earth. Let us hear it no more, but come to business at once."

Toohoolhoolzote glared at the one-armed soldier and snorted. The old man would not be silenced. He knew the Indians approved of what he said.

"You white people," he growled, "get together, measure the earth and then divide it....We never have made any trade." The speaker gestured toward the reservation Indians. "Part of the Indians gave up their land," he said, with a contemptuous sweep of the hand, as if he would like to sweep the reservation Indians out of existence. "I never did. The earth is part of my body, and I never gave up the earth."

"You know very well," Howard attempted, "that the government has set apart a reservation and that the Indians must go upon it....The government has set apart this large reservation for you and your children, that you may live in peace, and prosper."

Toohoolhoolzote was not impressed. He crossed his arms and shifted on his feet and muttered something angrily: "Who are you, that you ask us to talk, and then tell me I shan't talk? Are you the Great Spirit? Did you make the rivers run for us to drink? Did you make the grass to grow? Did you make all these things, that you talk to us as though we were boys? If you did, then you have the right to talk as you do."

Howard noticed a few heads nodding in agreement. "What did he say?" the general snapped at the interpreter.

"He demands," the interpreter replied, "'What person pretends to divide the land and put me on it?'"

Howard drew himself up indignantly. "I am the man," he boomed. "I stand here for the president, and there is no spirit good or bad that will hinder me."

The Indians stirred and mumbled angrily. Now it was White Bird's turn to speak. He was an old medicine man, a chief from the Salmon River gold regions, and his people had seen their share of trouble with the whites. White Bird looked at Howard sternly. He held an eagle's wing up to his nose; it was a symbol of his power. Before he spoke he folded the wing against his side, as if he thought he was the bird.

"If I had been taught from early life to be governed by the white men I would be governed by the white men. The earth rules me," White Bird said.

"Then you do not propose to comply with the orders of the government?" Howard moved forward threateningly.

Toohoolhoolzote answered him. "So long as the earth keeps me, I want to be left alone. You are trifling with the law of the earth."

Howard was beginning to understand that he could not intimidate Toohoolhoolzote, so he decided to change his ap-

Chief White Bird.
(Montana Historical Society,
Helena.)

proach. "Our old friend does not seem to understand," he began, "that the question is: Will the Indians come peaceably on the reservation, or do they want me, in compliance with my orders, to put them there by force?"

"I never gave the Indians authority to give away my lands," the Indian replied.

"Do you speak for yourself alone?" Howard demanded.

Toohoolhoolzote stopped for a moment. "The Indians may do what they like," he barked at Howard, "but I am not going on the reservation."

This gave Howard an opening. Now he could treat the old man as a troublemaker, not as a representative of the others. "This bad advice is what you give the Indians," he screeched. "On account of it, you will have to be taken to the Indian

Territory. Joseph and White Bird seem to have good hearts, but yours is bad. I will send you there if it takes years and years...."

The Indians' eyes widened in alarm as Howard threatened and scolded their speaker. The Indian Territory was a place far away where the whites sent Indians who'd been defeated in war. It was a terrible place, a hot, barren land where the Indians only withered and died from disease.

Now Howard turned to the others. "Will Joseph and White Bird and Looking-Glass go with me to look after their land? The old man shall not go. He must stay with Captain Perry."

The general called out for assistance and then, unable to wait for it, he himself grabbed the old man by the arm. Captain Perry hurried forward to help the general. Together the two men forced the Indian out of the tent and across the grounds to the guardhouse. Toohoolhoolzote made no effort to resist.

"My men whispered among themselves whether they should let this thing be done," Joseph recalled. "I counseled them to submit. I knew if we resisted that all the white men present, including General Howard, would be killed in a moment, and we would be blamed."

Howard and Perry handed Toohoolhoolzote over to a guard and then returned to the council tent. Howard faced the remaining chiefs and asked them if they were ready to pick out their land on the reservation. At first no one replied. Then one by one the chiefs agreed.

As Joseph explained: "I said in my heart that, rather than have a war, I would give up my country. I would give up my father's grave. I would give up everything rather than have the blood of white men upon the hands of my people."

The Blood
of White Men

Howard gave the Indians 30 days to move onto the reservation, an impossible order. The task required six months, not one. The Wallowas' horses and cattle were scattered across the hills and valleys, many of them with young too feeble to be moved. The rivers were flooding and dangerous to cross, and Howard knew this: one of his men had been swept from his horse and drowned trying to cross the Grande Ronde River.

The Indians' food supplies were low too. They needed time to gather roots and harvest fish. Joseph pleaded for more time, but Howard would not extend the deadline even a day.

The Indians were dispirited and angry. When Joseph and the others made it back to Wallowa, Howard's soldiers had already taken over the valley. The Indians who had stayed behind had waited anxiously for Joseph's return; now the people were thrown into confusion.

It was hard to understand this sudden loss. This country had sustained them all their lives, and now they had to give it up. How could the people survive without the land they loved?

They knew they would live like prisoners on the Idaho reservation, unable to hunt or fish beyond its borders, unable to leave without permission, unable to dig roots or pick berries in the highlands in the summer, or to drive their herds into the shelter of the canyons in the fall. The future looked bleak, and their hearts rebelled. Talk of revenge swept through the camp.

Toohoolhoolzote had been released, and he brought his people south to join the Wallowas. He was angrier than ever.

As Joseph explained, "Toohoolhoolzote, who felt outraged by his imprisonment, talked for war, and made many of my young men willing to fight rather than be driven like dogs from the land where they were born. He declared that blood alone would wash out the disgrace General Howard had put upon him. It required a strong heart to stand up against such talk, but I urged my people to be quiet, and not to begin a war."

Ollokot and many of the elders supported Joseph, and although the talk was spirited, the warriors eventually agreed to follow the Wallowa chiefs' advice. The word spread from lodge to lodge: the people would not fight. They were told to gather up their stock. They were moving to the reservation.

It was spring. The earth was warming, blooming, coming back to life, but Joseph grieved. His men searched the hillsides and canyons for their animals and drove them back towards camp. The women prepared their belongings for packing.

When they had gathered all the animals they could find, the people headed east to the Imnaha River, with everything they owned strapped to their horses' backs. Then they followed the Imnaha River through the steep canyons to the Snake.

The Snake River was grey with foam. Its roar echoed on the walls of the canyon. The Indians moved away from the place where the two rivers joined and cut across a piece of rocky land, catching the Snake again further east. They were searching for a place to cross the river. Finally they found a spot where the river narrowed slightly, and the difficult task of crossing it began.

It took them two whole days. First a few young men guided their horses into the powerful current. The river swept them downstream in a long diagonal from bank to bank. They finally scrambled to safety on the opposite shore, trotted back up the river and signaled to their people: Yes, it could be done.

Everyone set to work, building boats for those too young or weak to cross on horseback. These bowl-shaped "bull-boats" were formed from curved slats lashed together with buffalo robes stretched over the frames. The boats were loaded with baggage and people at the water's edge. Three or four horse-men would guide each one across. It was dangerous work and the children clung in terror as their boats skipped and rocked downstream.

When almost everyone had made it safely across the river, the few remaining riders drove the horses and cattle into the flood. In wide-eyed terror the animals plunged ahead, paddling wildly for the opposite shore. The water was swift, and they bobbed and bumped into one another as they struggled. Once ashore, they quickly found their footing and dashed away from the water's edge, then stood together dripping and snorting and staring back toward the river as if they thought it might come after them.

But many of the horses and cattle never made it safely across. The river dragged them under and there was nothing anyone could do. At the end of the ordeal hundreds of animals had been lost.

After a rest the people drove forward along a creek that wound out of the canyons. They were on their way to a place called Tepahlewam. They still had two weeks before the deadline and they decided to spend these last days of freedom at the Tepahlewam camas grounds.

Eventually they made it to the Salmon River, the last obstacle before the camas grounds. Instead of driving their horses and cattle across the river, the people went on without them, leaving the animals in the care of a few herders.

Tepahlewam had always been a gathering place for the Indians. Each year when the blue camas flowers faded, the people flocked to the prairie to dig the camas bulbs, a food they ate year-round. All the different bands came to Tepahlewam each year, and they celebrated their reunion with games and feasts and competitions.

Most of the other bands from the council had already gathered there. It was camas-digging season, and this meeting place was not far from the reservation. Soon the women were rooting for camas bulbs, the men celebrating and parading as if nothing had changed. Joseph left the people there, and traveled back across the river to slaughter some cattle for the tribe. He took several people with him, including his oldest daughter and Ollokot and Ollokot's wife, Wetatonmi.

But while Joseph was away the mood in the camp began to change. The people could not forget that their days of freedom were running out. At night they laughed and wept and told their stories and talked of war. Each band had suffered countless insults and injustices from the whites, and as they remembered these events their grief and hatred were revived.

During the day the games and races took on a new spirit. The men competed fiercely, their anger at the whites sometimes directed at each other, their tempers short. They raced their horses between the lodges and fired their guns in the air. When evening closed around the camp, they chanted and danced around their fires. Late into the night their shrill cries trailed over the prairie.

Two days before the deadline the warriors stripped down to loincloths and painted themselves and paraded through the camp as if prepared for battle. They were playing at war, but the game wasn't satisfying. Instead of affirming their faith in themselves, the war songs, competitions and parades only reminded the people of their own lost strength. The show was a pretense, otherwise why were they letting the whites force them onto the reservation? As the days sped by, their humiliation grew.

And they could not forget the council. They had endured many wrongs, but this injury was too much to bear. Howard's haughty attitude at the meeting, his fierce demand that the Indians obey him, his insulting treatment of Toohoolhoolzote, and his unreasonable deadline all awakened the Indians' rage. They remembered all the past abuses in the light of Howard's actions. Their hope for justice had sustained them, but Howard had destroyed that hope. A young warrior of Joseph's band explained, "it was all because General Howard talked the rifle when in a peace council....The war grew from the rifle at council, and the big waters in the Snake and Salmon Rivers."

On the day of Howard's deadline the chiefs and elders gathered to discuss their situation. Someone shouted from a nearby lodge: "You poor people are talking for nothing. Three boys have already started war! They killed a white man on the Salmon and brought his horse to this camp. It is already war!"

Lahmotta

When Joseph returned the next morning he found the camp in chaos. An Indian named Two Moons met his party on the trail. "War has broke out!" he shouted. "Three white men killed yesterday!" In horror, Joseph hurried to the camp, hoping to prevent a panic.

He was too late. Most of the people had taken down their lodges and were gathering up their goods in haste. Some had already fled with their families. Others were arming themselves for a new attack against the whites. Joseph and Ollokot rushed from lodge to lodge, arguing with the people, begging them to reconsider. But the warriors turned away from the brothers in disgust. This was the talk of cowards, they insisted.

"I was deeply grieved," Joseph remembered. "All the lodges were moved except my brother's and my own. I saw clearly that the war was upon us when I learned that my young men had been secretly buying ammunition. I heard then that Toohoolhoolzote...had succeeded in organizing a war-party. I knew that their acts would involve all my people. I saw that the war could not then be prevented."

After a difficult night, Joseph and Ollokot decided to follow the fleeing bands. Joseph realized he could not abandon the warriors now. He hated this war, but he would join it, for the Nez Perces were a family. Joseph, Ollokot and their followers gathered up their things and trailed across the prairie to meet the other Indians in a large cave they called Sapachesap.

The young men of the other bands had already made several raids against the settlers. Joseph was horrified when he learned about these attacks. At first the braves had only gone after settlers who'd committed crimes against their people, but the violence quickly flared out of control. Innocent settlers became victims along with the guilty. The warriors murdered women and children. They stole whiskey and, in their drunkenness, committed acts that made even the elders shudder.

"I would have given my own life if I could have undone the killing of white men by my people," Joseph said. "I know that my young men did a great wrong, but I ask, who was first to blame? They had been insulted a thousand times; their fathers and mothers had been killed; their mothers and wives had been disgraced; they had been driven to madness by whiskey sold to them by white men; they had been told by General Howard that all their horses and cattle which they had been unable to drive out of Wallowa were to fall into the hands of white men; and, added to all this, they were homeless and desperate....

"If General Howard had given me plenty of time to gather up my stock, and treated Toohoolhoolzote as a man should be treated, there would have been no war."

The headmen finally decided to move away from the white settlements. As long as they remained in familiar territory their people were at risk. The young warriors could not be controlled, and their reckless attacks endangered everyone. If the Indians stayed in one place the soldiers would soon overtake them. They had to keep moving, they had to flee, but where would they go?

Panorama of White Bird Canyon. (Historical Photograph Collections, Washington State University Libraries, Negative 92-166.)

First they headed down the south fork of the Clearwater River past the white settlements of Mt. Idaho. Then they left the river and made their way west to White Bird Creek. Finally they decided they would be safest among the rolling steeps of White Bird Canyon — a place they called Lahmotta.

At last the people came to a bluff that overlooked the canyon. The earth swept down from the ridge where they stood, revealing a land that buckled and rolled. The highest ridges of the canyon jutted up like bony shoulders, but in the valleys the little hills and buttes were gently sloped. Everything was blanketed with grass. Beyond the hills a line of icy mountain ridges edged the sky. A few clouds puffed above the hills.

The people found a campsite in the bottom of the canyon on White Bird Creek, put up their lodges and moved the stock to a grassy spot so the animals could graze. Dozens of horses were taken out of the herd and hitched to stakes close to camp. These were the war-horses, kept nearby in case of an attack.

The sun soon dropped behind the mountains, and darkness overtook the camp. The air was crisp and full of sound.

Crickets chanted and a few frogs barked from the creek bottoms. Some men were drinking whiskey and talking loudly at one end of the camp, but most of the people were quiet. An uneasy peace had settled in.

But the tranquility lasted only a few hours. Shortly after midnight the people were awakened by the sound of horses galloping into the camp. The scouts had hurried in from their outposts to warn the chiefs: they had seen a hundred soldiers moving in to occupy a ridge above the canyon.

The chiefs quickly got together to discuss what they would do. Still hoping to avoid a war, they decided that when the soldiers first approached they would send six men forward with a flag of truce. "Ollokot told the Indians not to fire first," one of the warriors recalled. "He wanted to learn the intentions of the soldiers."

But the Indians also prepared themselves for battle. The old men and the women and children drove the herds to a protected place behind the camp. Just before dawn the warriors stripped themselves down to their loincloths and moved among the rocks and crags and waited for daylight.

There were only 60 men ready for a fight. Many of the others had made themselves drunk and would be useless in a battle. Most of the braves were poorly armed. If fighting did erupt they would have to defend themselves with bows and arrows and ancient muskets and shotguns. Only a few carried rifles like those the whites would use.

The soldiers appeared at dawn, as expected, atop a ridge that overlooked the camp. Nine men on horseback first cleared the ridge, followed closely by their scouts, who were Indians from the reservation. Meanwhile the warriors in the canyon mounted their horses and waited as their men moved forward with the white flag. One of the soldiers signaled to an unseen force beyond the ridge, and soon the rest of the troops appeared. Most were in uniform, but another, smaller group was not. The men in this group were volunteers, settlers and ranchers who'd chosen to help the soldiers fight the Indians.

The soldiers would have done better without such help. The volunteers were difficult to control, and often they were undisciplined and cowardly. Anxious to fight, but courageous only when the enemy was outnumbered, the volunteers often behaved more like a mob than like soldiers. To make matters worse, some of these men had come seeking revenge.

Unfortunately it was a volunteer named Arthur Chapman who saw the white flag first. Before the military command could send out an order, Chapman pointed his rifle at the flag and fired twice. Hearing the gunshots, one of the warriors aimed his rifle at the soldiers' bugler and pulled the trigger. The bugler collapsed — killed by the Indian's bullet. Immediately the hills exploded with gunfire.

The white commander depended on his bugler to issue his commands. Now he had to run his horse up and down the lines, shouting directions to his men. With one bullet one Indian had disabled the entire American force.

The Indians were not bound to follow the instructions of any one man. Each warrior chose to fight as he saw fit, acting alone or with a group. Several braves would often follow a particular leader for a while, but each man was responsible to no one but himself. He might distinguish himself through acts of bravery, but he could also choose not to fight.

The American soldier, however, could never act on his own. He was expected to follow the directions of his superiors. If he disagreed with his commander or refused to follow orders, he would be punished. The commander was the brain of the operation; the soldiers provided only muscle.

The soldier's training made him effective in some ways, but it also gave the Indian an advantage. The warrior could see for himself what needed to be done and respond immediately. The soldiers usually advanced in wide lines, sometimes at a great distance from their commanders, as though the hands were somehow separate from the brain. Their movements were slow and often predictable.

As the fighting continued, the whites formed a line and tried to advance, but the Indians attacked from all sides. The soldiers in the middle of the line dismounted, and their horses were led away to safety beyond the ridge. The volunteers extended the left end of the soldiers' line.

Suddenly a bunch of Indians appeared atop a bluff. When they charged, the terrified volunteers retreated. Another group of Indians emerged from the brush and, firing and wailing, galloped toward the mounted soldiers on the opposite end of the line. Some of the soldiers' horses panicked and bolted. The men on foot rushed for their mounts. The line was gone.

The soldiers panicked. A few riderless horses ran around in confused circles. Soon the white men scattered in all directions.

The Indians were relentless. They chased the men into ravines and over buttes and hills and overtook them and cut them down. When the battle was over 34 soldiers had been slain. Their bodies lay where they had fallen. The Indians stole their guns and ammunition and made their way back to the camp, exuberant. Not one of their men had fallen in the battle.

A Clever Escape

A panic swept across the countryside. Whole settlements were abandoned, the families fleeing in wagons to the larger towns. The missionary at Kamiah at the east end of the reservation hurried to the safety of the garrison at Lapwai. Miners evacuated their mines, farmers left their farms, stockmen deserted the open range. No one knew where the Indians would show up next.

When he heard of the soldiers' defeat, General Howard immediately wired for more troops from every part of the western territory. The soldiers set out for Idaho from California, Oregon, Washington state, even Alaska. Volunteers were also recruited for the effort. Eventually Howard moved all his men down to the head of White Bird Canyon, and he picked up more volunteers at every stop along the way.

Nine days had passed since the first battle, and the Indians had already crossed the Salmon River. The military scouts had seen them on the distant hills beyond it.

Howard sent some of his men into White Bird Canyon to bury the dead. The corpses of the slain men were scattered across the hills, their bodies bloated and their faces "blackening in the sun." The soldiers buried them in shallow pits covered with mounds of stones to keep the coyotes from digging them up. At a few of the rock piles they hung the dead men's hats on sticks as markers. There was no other way to identify the graves.

Meanwhile the Indians had decided they would be safest in the mountains on the far side of the river. If Howard followed them, they could recross the Salmon at another spot and escape.

Howard set out after the Indians had already moved into the mountains, and he soon realized it would not be easy to navigate the river. He had to get hundreds of men and a howitzer cannon across the flood, along with all his supplies, ammunition, horses and pack animals. Unlike the Indians, the soldiers were unable to ride their animals across the river, and several boats had to be brought downstream. A heavy rope, anchored on both shores, was stretched above the torrent. The men hoped to use a pulley to guide the boats along the rope. They spent a day and a half working to secure the line, then discovered their only pulley didn't work. Slowly, laboriously, they rowed the boats back and forth across the river.

But the nightmare had only begun. Once across the river they faced an even more difficult task: following the Indians' trail. As one of Howard's men put it in a letter to his wife, the countryside over which the Indians had traveled was "broken beyond...description — a perfect sea of mountains, gullies, ravines, canyons." The Indians had followed a course that ran almost vertically up the mountain through a dense clutter of trees and forest growth and fallen logs. To make matters worse, it rained most of that first day and the rain continued into the night. By morning the men were drenched and the trail had turned into a muddy bog. Some of the pack animals lost their footing on the steep course and fell down the mountainside into the canyon below, carrying their baggage with them.

The men soon came upon the Indians' first camp along a stream called Deer Creek. Here they found that the Indians had buried hundreds of pounds of food and other items too heavy to haul across the mountains. Much of the abandoned cargo had been stolen from the white settlers in the first days of the war. In similar fashion, the packers and soldiers helped themselves to all the loot they could carry.

But Howard and his men were following a cold trail. The Indians had already recrossed the Salmon at a place called Craig's Ferry and were heading east, away from the river. Two days later, when Howard reached Craig's Ferry, he could not get across the river. The Indians had outmaneuvered him. He and his men would have to retrace every step over the mountain.

The Clearwater

It seemed there were soldiers everywhere. The day after the Indians crossed the river, a warrior named Seeyakoon Ilppilp (Red Spy) rode into camp with news that a group of soldiers was camped nearby. Several warriors immediately mounted their horses and set out for higher ground. From a ridge above the prairie they could see the soldiers' camp: a cluster of canvas tents set up near the Cottonwood River. The warriors got off their horses and stripped themselves for battle. Soon they saw a line of soldiers approaching on horseback. This was the cavalry.

"We attacked them," Joseph recalled, "killing one officer, two guides, and ten men."

The Indians withdrew for the night, and the surviving soldiers returned to their camp, carrying their dead.

"We withdrew, hoping the soldiers would follow," Joseph explained, "but they had got fighting enough for that day. They entrenched themselves, and next day we attacked them again. The battle lasted all day, and was renewed the next morning."

But the Indians wanted to move on and, while the warriors distracted the soldiers, the families drove their herds around the soldiers' camp and headed east. One of the warriors was severely wounded and died. His name was Weesculatat, the first Indian killed in the Nez Perce War.

The Indians set up camp near the South Fork of the Clearwater River. Soon they were joined by another band of Nez Perces, led by a chief named Looking Glass. Looking Glass told the other chiefs that soldiers had attacked his village even though his men had put up a white flag of truce when they saw the soldiers approaching. The soldiers had sprayed the village with gunfire as the men, women and children fled for their lives. Several people were wounded. One woman ran with her child into the river where they both drowned. The soldiers then tore up the Indians' abandoned lodges and gardens and stole several hundred horses.

"Of course that settled it," an Indian said. "We had to have a war."

Now there were five bands of Nez Perces gathered at the Clearwater camp, and five headmen to lead them: Joseph, White Bird, Toohoolhoolzote, Looking Glass, and another chief named Husishusis Kute. There were about 250 warriors, and more than 500 women and children. Each band operated more or less independently, looking to its own chief for guidance.

Chief Joseph was the youngest of the headmen. Unlike the others, he had never been in a war. Although he used his rifle on a few occasions, he didn't like to fight. So the other chiefs asked him to care for the families, to guide the women and children out of danger. It was a task of great importance, and Joseph devoted himself to it wholeheartedly.

"Joseph had not the fighting blood in him," a young brave later explained, "as none of his ancestors were warriors."

For several days, the Indian camp on the Clearwater was calm. Some of the young men raced their horses along the river while others cooled off with a swim. The blistering sun scorched everything. A few children played at the water's edge, digging in the mud with sticks. In camp the cooking fires blazed, sending up little spirals of black smoke. Most of the people lounged around the lodges, unwilling to exert themselves in the dizzying heat.

One afternoon a strange sound cracked the sky. It came from the bluffs on the east side of the river. The people looked up at the hills. They had not expected soldiers from that direction. They had left Howard and the other soldiers in the *west* and so their scouts had only looked to the west for signs of danger.

"Soldiers appeared on the mountain about a mile and a half to the north," Ollokot's wife, Wetatonmi remembered. "A puff of smoke was seen, then came a cannon's boom." A 4-inch cannon shell flew over the camp. Howard's forces had arrived.

The men sprang into action. "I saw the warriors stripping for the battle," Wetatonmi continued. "I saw a bunch of them, mounted and led by Chief Toohoolhoolzote, run their horses a ways up the river, where they crossed and climbed the mountain to meet the soldiers. Soon there was fighting up there, and the guns were heard plainly."

Howard's forces had taken the village by surprise, but the warriors managed to hold them off until dark even though they were outnumbered by more than four to one. But the next afternoon, when cavalry arrived with supplies for Howard, the Indians could no longer keep the soldiers from plunging forward toward the edge of the bluff. The warriors tumbled down the mountainside and across the river into the camp.

Down in the camp, the families were not prepared to flee. Some of the women had cooking fires going when they saw the warriors rushing down from the hills. Suddenly a storm of gunfire enveloped their village. Soldiers were charging down the mountain and firing into the camp. Women grabbed children and mounted horses and raced away from the noise. Some of the people tried to herd the scattering animals.

"The...soldiers charged upon us," Joseph said, "and we retreated with our families and stock a few miles, leaving 80 lodges to fall into General Howard's hands."

Howard's soldiers did not follow the Indians beyond their abandoned camp. Instead they set upon the treasures the Indians had left behind.

The Lolo Trail

Looking Glass told the Indians they should retreat into Montana. They had many white friends in the buffalo country, he said, who would not want to join Howard's war. They could move into the area, proclaiming that they had left the war behind them. Surely, he said, the whites would want to leave the Indians alone.

Once they made it to Montana the people could head east to the land of the Crow Indians. Looking Glass said the Crows would welcome the Nez Perces. And if the soldiers followed them, the Crows might even join the war. Or the people could flee into Canada, as Sitting Bull had done, leaving the Americans on the other side of the border. After a few years the Indians might even be able to return to their homes, he said.

The war chiefs liked the idea, and so it was agreed. They decided to take the Lolo Trail, a path that led over the Bitterroot Mountains and into Montana. The chiefs spread the word from lodge to lodge, telling the young men to behave themselves in Montana; they could not afford to make new enemies in the buffalo country.

Joseph was not completely satisfied with this decision. He felt his people were already too far from home. The Wallowas were homesick, and he could not see the sense in dragging them to Montana. But he could not dissuade the others, so he was forced to go along. He had no choice but to abide by the decision of the majority. If he and Ollokot abandoned the fight, Howard might have them hanged as war leaders. For the moment he and his people would have to stay with the other bands. But the further they got from the Wallowa country, the more despondent Joseph became.

The people drove the horses forward over the hills, through the tangle of fallen trees that "crossed and crisscrossed" the Lolo Trail. Two respected warriors, Rainbow and Five Wounds, had just returned from the buffalo country over this trail when they discovered their people were at war. Now, with Looking Glass, they were leading the Indians back over the Bitterroot Mountains into Montana.

Howard's soldiers tried to follow them, but a rear guard of warriors ambushed and killed some of the soldiers' Nez Perce scouts. After that the people were not bothered from behind.

It took them nine days to get across the mountains, driving their animals up the winding course and over the difficult terrain. Finally the trail began to weave back down the mountain and the people prepared to descend into the valley that marked the end of the trail. But before they got very far their scouts returned to announce that a detachment of *Montana* soldiers blocked their path.

Looking Glass was not afraid of the Montana soldiers, and he and White Bird and Joseph rode down the mountain to talk to them. The whites were amazed to see the chiefs approach them in such a friendly manner. The Indians even laughed at the crude barricades the soldiers had hastily built. Then the chiefs told the white commander, Captain Charles C. Rawn, that if he would allow them to pass into Montana, they would move on without disturbance.

Rawn said he would let them pass only if they turned over all their weapons. The Indians refused. White Bird remembered a white commander who had hanged many Indians from western tribes after convincing them to surrender their weapons. Besides, the chiefs argued, the men would need their guns for hunting buffalo in the north.

The Indians met with Rawn three times, but could come to no agreement.

"They said, 'You can not get by us,'" Joseph recalled. "We answered, 'We are going by you without fighting if you will let us, but we are going by you anyhow.'"

Instead of continuing down the mountain towards the valley, the Indians blazed a new path on higher ground, and moved around the soldiers' barricades to escape. Many of Rawn's volunteers, upon hearing that the Indians would not attack unless provoked, abandoned the barricades. Although a few shots were fired, by the time Rawn was ready to charge after the fleeing Indians, he did not have enough men left to do the job. Once again the Indians had gotten around the American forces.

Arrogance

The next night some of Rawn's volunteers accidentally stumbled upon the Indian camp in the Bitterroot Valley. The white men were frightened, but Looking Glass quickly assured them that his people wanted no trouble. "I give you my word of honor that I will harm nobody," Looking Glass declared.

"We then made a treaty with these soldiers," Joseph said. "We agreed not to molest anyone, and they agreed that we might pass through the Bitterroot country in peace."

The white men went on their way, thankful that the Indians had not opted for revenge.

Soon whites throughout the valley learned of the Nez Perces' pledge of peace, and many came out of hiding, trusting that the Indians would keep their word. In Stevensville, some of the merchants even opened their stores, and the Indians came in to buy flour, sugar, tobacco and other items.

The exchange went well until an Indian got drunk on some whiskey one of the storekeepers had sold him. Looking Glass had the Indian dragged back into camp and guarded until he was sober. After that the chief marched up and down the streets of Stevensville to make sure none of his men got into trouble.

Chief Looking Glass. (Smithsonian Institution Photo No. 2953-A.)

After two days in the Stevensville area the Indians continued south, stopping at Corvallis and Skalkaho, where they
also traded openly with the whites and even visited some settlers
in their homes. There was no sign that Howard's men were

coming after them. But as they moved on up the valley some of the warriors raided a settler's home, stealing some food and a few items of clothing. Looking Glass made the Indians take three horses to the white man's house, brand the animals with the man's branding iron, and leave them behind as payment for the damage they had done.

This behavior was unusual for a chief. Normally a headman had no authority to punish his men. The Indians respected a person's right to do as he pleased. A wrongdoer might be shamed or shunned by the rest of the band, but was rarely forced to pay for his misdeeds. Looking Glass's approach was more like the justice of the whites.

But the people were in a difficult situation. As they moved into unfamiliar territory they became more and more dependent on the war chief. Only Looking Glass and the other buffalo hunters knew with certainty where they were going. The others simply had to follow. As long as the people relied on Looking Glass for guidance, they had to put up with his overbearing manner.

As he brought them up the valley, some of the people began to feel anxious. They felt they were advancing too slowly. Looking Glass had them moving only 12 to 15 miles a day. Many worried that the soldiers would come after them. A sense of foreboding settled over the camp. A few of the men had dreams of death in battle, and they warned the others of their visions.

"I will be killed soon!" a warrior named Wahlitits cried as he rode through the camp one morning. "I do not care. I am willing to die.... I shall not turn back from death. We are all going to die!"

Another man tried to get the chiefs to alter their plan, predicting catastrophe if the people did not pick up the pace.

"My shaking heart tells me trouble and death will overtake us if we make no hurry through this land!...We should keep going!...Move fast! Death may now be following on our trail!"

But Looking Glass laughed at them and said they were worrying for nothing.

Some of the other headmen were dissatisfied with Looking Glass's leadership. They were used to making decisions as a group, preferring to draw upon the wisdom of several men, not the experience of just one. This had always been their strength.

Looking Glass upset this process. But his experience as a war hero and his solid confidence in himself finally convinced the others. They decided to let him lead as he saw fit.

"All right, Looking Glass," Five Wounds said when the chief would not allow him to scout around to see if the Indians were being followed, "You are one of the chiefs! I have no wife, no children to be placed fronting the danger that I feel coming to us. Whatever the gains, whatever the loss, it is yours."

Young mothers. (Idaho State Historical Society #63-221.126.)

The Big Hole

The Indians intended to go peaceably to the buffalo country and remain there, leaving the question of returning to their homeland to be settled later. The Indians were tired of the conflict, weary from traveling. They did not want any more war.

"With this understanding we traveled on for four days," Joseph recalled, "and, thinking that the trouble was all over, we stopped and prepared tent-poles to take with us. We started again, and at the end of two days we saw three white men passing our camp. Thinking that peace had been made, we did not molest them. We could have killed or taken them prisoners, but we did not suspect them of being spies, which they were."

A white colonel named John Gibbon had been trailing the Indians and had finally caught up with them. Later the same night he ordered his soldiers to surround the sleeping Nez Perce camp.

The next morning, while it was still dark, he sent some men to scatter the Indian herd before ordering an advance. The animals were grazing quietly on the hillside without a guard.

The sky brightened as the soldiers moved slowly down the mountain. Gibbon's men advanced from three directions, pick-

Yellow Wolf.
(Montana Historical
Society, Helena.)

ing their way through the trees and out into the open marsh. Gibbon had ordered them to attack the Indians as they slept.

As the soldiers moved forward, they spotted an old Indian man coming out of one of the lodges. The soldiers halted and stood completely motionless as the old man mounted his horse. They watched as he headed straight for their line. It was clear he had not seen them. He started toward the mountain to check the herd.

The old man's eyesight was bad but as he approached the stream that lay between the mountain and the camp, he began to sense that something was terribly wrong. He stopped his horse and leaned forward, listening to every sound and peering at the shadowy line that seemed to spread out across the marsh...Soldiers!

The line burst into fire, and the old man toppled from his horse. The soldiers yelled and dashed forward, firing and running for the camp. The Indians were startled awake by the terrible noise.

"I was half sleeping," Chief Joseph's nephew, Yellow Wolf said. "I lay with eyes closed. Maybe I was dreaming? I did not think what to do! Then I was awake. I heard rapidly about four gunshots across there to the west...This gunfire made me wide awake."

All at once a storm engulfed the camp.

"I heard bullets ripping the tepee walls," one man, a child at the time, remembered, "pattering like raindrops."

Many died inside their lodges in those first moments. Others, still dazed by sleep, got outside only to fall in the hail of gunfire.

Gibbon watched as his men "plunged into the stream and climbed up the opposite bank, shooting down the startled Indians as they rushed from their tents pell-mell, men, women and children together."

The warriors rushed for their guns. Chief Joseph stumbled out of his tepee and scrambled up the mountainside to save the horses. He didn't have time to dress. One of the warriors saw him running barefoot and without his leggings.

The roar of the battle was deafening. Some warriors stood just outside their lodges and fired at the advancing men. When the women and children came out, they had no idea which way to run.

"Soldiers...came rushing among the tepees," a boy remembered. "Bullets flying everywhere....It was like spurts of fire, lightning all around." The confused, defenseless women and children scattered.

A few of the women grabbed youngsters and rushed to the river to hide in the water. Others plunged into the brush or charged between the fighting men to get away. Some were killed as they ran with their children in their arms.

The warriors fought aggressively and got around some of the soldiers.

"They shot down on us like a hailstorm, but we faced it, charging toward them," a Nez Perce named Husis Owyeen (Wounded in Head) recalled. "Hand to hand, club to club. All mixed up, warriors and soldiers fought. It was a bloody battle."

Small holes began to appear in the soldiers' line, and the people hurried through. They climbed the hills and hid among the trees and waited as soldiers poured into the camp.

About this time Joseph ran into a warrior named Two Moons. After collecting the horses, Joseph had come back down the mountain for his family. He was holding his baby daughter, shielding her with his body. He told Two Moons he had no gun.

"Skip for your life," Two Moons advised him. "Without the gun you can do nothing. Save the child!"

The two men looked back toward the camp and saw it burning. The soldiers had set some of the tepees on fire.

"Little children were in some of those tepees," an Indian woman later reported. "Sleeping in blankets, they were burned to death."

Finally the warriors managed to drive the soldiers back up the hill. "There the warriors kept them all that day and all night," an Indian named Eelahweemah remembered.

The camp was now clear of fighting, and the women and children left their hiding places and wandered back. Joseph and some of the other men brought the horses in so that the families

The route of war

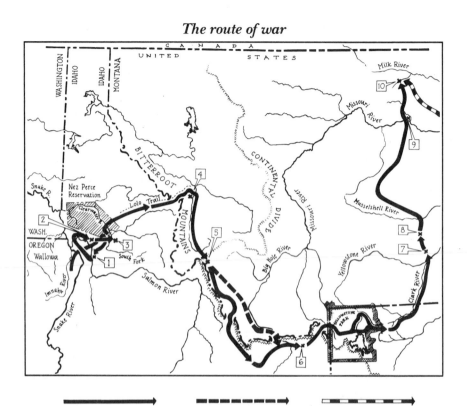

Route of Nez Perces   Howard's route   Col. Nelson Miles

1. **June 17.** Battle of White Bird Canyon.

2. **July 1-8.** Nez Perces outmaneuver Howard at Salmon River.

3. **July 11-12.** Battle of the Clearwater River.

4. **July 28.** Nez Perces get around blockade at end of Lolo Trail.

5. **Aug. 9.** Battle at Big Hole.

6. **Aug. 20.** Warriors steal Howard's mules at Camas Meadows.

7. **Sept. 8-29.** Nez Perces hurry north.

8. Crows and Bannocks chase fleeing Nez Perce families.

9. **Sept. 23.** Nez Perces cross Missouri River.

10. **Sept. 30-Oct. 5.** Battle of Bear Paws.

could pack up their belongings and escape. The bodies of soldiers and Indians lay strewn in clusters around the lodges and along the river. The people moved among the dead and tried to understand what had happened.

"We lost 50 women and children and 30 fighting men," Joseph said. "We remained long enough to bury our dead. The Nez Perces never make war on women and children; we could have killed a great many women and children while the war lasted, but we would have been ashamed to do so cowardly an act."

"They all cried when they saw what had been done," an Indian named Red Elk recalled. "Boys, girls, women and children, and men who had no guns, no arms, lay scattered among dead soldiers, burned tepees, and bedding."

Many women and children had been slain, as well as some of the most honored warriors. Wahlitits, who had envisioned his own death, had been killed, along with his wife. Rainbow, whose spirit-power would protect him only in a battle begun after sunrise, now lay dead.

When Five Wounds, Rainbow's closest companion, came upon his friend lying dead he cried: "My brother has passed away. I too will now go, as did his father and my father die in war. They lay side by side where the battle was strongest. And now I shall lay down beside my brother war-mate. He is no more, and I shall see that I follow him." When they heard this the other warriors knew Five Wounds would not live to see another sunrise.

The terrible work of identifying the dead continued for some time. A few of the women searched for lost children and found their husbands slain as well. They fell upon the bodies and wept.

The wounded were also crying. The air was full of the sound of weeping. Some were badly hurt and needed immediate care. Yellow Wolf remembered: "Wounded children screaming with pain. Women and men crying, wailing for their scattered dead! The air was heavy with sorrow. I would not want to hear, I would not want to see, again."

But there wasn't time to mourn for those who had fallen. The soldiers could not be held off indefinitely. The able-bodied hurried to care for the wounded and to bury the dead. Most of the Indians' belongings would be left behind in the rush. There was only so much they could do.

Joseph moved among the families and tried to help them prepare to leave. He helped the women and men drag their dead down to the river where they wedged the bodies into hollows along the shore. With bare hands he helped them pull the loose earth down from the eroded riverbank to cover the dead.

The badly wounded were loaded onto litters hitched to the horses' backs, some of the lodges were pulled down, and at noon the people headed out, burdened with grief for those they left behind. Each family had lost at least one member in the fight.

While the warriors kept the soldiers busy on the hill, Joseph, White Bird and a few fighting men led the families and the herds south, away from the battle. They moved as quickly as they could, though they were overwhelmed with sadness and uncertainty about the future. They kept moving until they could no longer hear the sound of gunfire popping on the hills around the Big Hole.

"All along that trail was crying," an Indian named Black Eagle said. "Mourning for many left where we thought no war would come. Old people, half-grown boys and girls, mothers and little babies. Many only half-buried — left for wolves and coyotes. I can never forget that day."

Bitterness

In one day everything had changed for Joseph's people. They could no longer trust the white settlers to keep out of Howard's war.

"Through the Bitterroot Valley they spied on us while selling us vegetables, groceries, anything we wanted," Yellow Wolf said. "They spied on us crossing the mountains when we thought not of foes....Had some of the chiefs not thought all war ended for sure, we would not have been caught as we were."

Chief Joseph brooded silently as he marched with his people and tried to attend to their needs. The wounded had to be dragged on litters hitched to the backs of their horses, and the rough ride caused them terrible pain. The Indians had few pieces of cloth with which they could bind their wounds. Many died from their injuries and had to be buried on the trail. Others begged to be left behind.

As the days crawled by Joseph grew afraid that nothing but misery lay ahead. And as they saw their people dying on the trail after the fight, the warriors' grief hardened into hatred. Some of the young braves were ready to shoot any white man they encountered. In those first days several innocent men were attacked simply because they stumbled across the Indians' path.

Yellowstone National Park. (Historical Photograph Collections, Washington State University Libraries, Negative No. 70-0246.)

"The Indians were getting bad," Yellow Wolf observed. "The chiefs could no longer restrain them."

The people moved south out of the Big Hole country across a wide valley. Small groups of warriors ranged across the land, scouting for soldiers and stealing horses. Several more white men died in skirmishes with these raiders. The warriors also broke into some homes, stealing cloth for bandages and other items that could be used to treat the wounded.

Then the bands moved south across the mountains, re-entering Idaho. They were trying to make it to Yellowstone National Park before the soldiers overtook them. Then they would pass through the park to the buffalo country beyond.

Looking Glass had been disgraced as a leader by the surprise at Big Hole, but the Indians stuck to their original plan. Now a hunter-warrior named Poker Joe guided them. Poker Joe was half French, half Nez Perce. He had joined the bands shortly after their arrival in Montana. He was also known as Lean Elk,

Riders with war poles.
(Idaho State Historical
Society #63-221.18.)

Little Tobacco, and Hototo, but earned the name "Poker Joe" because he loved to play poker. Rainbow, Five Wounds and most of the other hunters who might have led the Indians had died at Big Hole. Poker Joe's bravery and knowledge of Montana convinced the chiefs to follow him. Now the Indians' fate lay in the hands of a man who loved to gamble.

But Poker Joe was a wiser leader than Looking Glass. He tried to keep the warriors under control, but he did not force them to obey him. He told the people to move quickly, because he knew the soldiers would come after them.

The Indians hurried on toward Yellowstone Park, keeping south of the imposing mountains. Just as they prepared to cross the mountains into the park, their scouts discovered soldiers following closely on their trail. General Howard had finally made it to the scene, bringing with him several hundred fighting men. The soldiers had set up camp only 15 miles behind the Indians.

That night some of the warriors sneaked into the soldiers' herd and began cutting the animals loose. They hoped to drive the horses off so Howard and his men would be unable to follow their trail, but the soldiers discovered the warriors before the job was done. Fighting broke out and continued for several hours before the Indians retreated to their camp. The warriors discovered that in the darkness they had mistakenly freed Howard's mules instead of his horses. But the soldiers did not follow them; Howard's men were worn out from the chase.

Two days after their brush with Howard, the Indians made it through an opening in the mountains and continued east to Yellowstone National Park. The chiefs had planned to take the traditional Nez Perce trail across the park, but Poker

Joe convinced them to take a shorter route. Howard's Bannock scouts were following them closely, and the sooner they made it out of Yellowstone the better.

As they hurried across the park, they stumbled upon a number of tourists. Poker Joe and the other chiefs wanted the tourists to be held safely, even released, but many of the warriors were full of rage from the slaughter at Big Hole, and killed some of them.

Later, as they scouted around the park, some warriors came upon a cabin. A man was standing in the doorway. The warriors had traveled quite a distance from the main camp, and this man represented little threat. But the Indians still thirsted for revenge for what had happened at Big Hole.

As they sat on their horses and stared at the white man one of them said, "My two young brothers and my next younger brother were not warriors. They and a sister were killed at Big Hole. It was just like this man that did the killing of my brothers and sister. He is nothing but a killer to become a soldier sometime. We are going to kill him now. I am a man! I am going to shoot him! When I fire, you shoot after me."

The warriors' anguish over their losses at Big Hole made them feel their actions were justified. If women and children were to be slain, the warriors reasoned, then so too would innocent whites. After all, was it not worse to attack whole families while they slept than to kill a man who could help the enemy? As long as the war continued, the warriors decided, there could be no other justice than this.

The Indian aimed his rifle and fired, hitting the stranger in the arm. The man tried to run away and another Indian shot him in the belly. The white man fell, and the Indians left him there to die.

America Loves
a Winner

General Howard was in trouble. In the first few weeks of the war the Indians had crushed his forces at White Bird Canyon, eluded him at the Salmon River, passed Whipple's men, escaped from both the Clearwater and Big Hole battlefields, slid around Rawn's blockade, and raided the general's camp, making off with his mules. Now they had made it into Yellowstone National Park. Hundreds of fighting men had been enlisted, hundreds of thousands of dollars had been spent, and many soldiers and volunteers had died in battles with the Indians. Howard had been trailing the Nez Perces for two months and still had not brought the war to a successful close.

The general's superiors had lost confidence in him. Newspapers across the nation had printed every detail of the hapless chase, and public opinion was quickly mounting against the American forces. In fact, as the war dragged on, more and more people began to identify with the *Indians'* cause. Chief Joseph was thought to be the leader of the warring bands, and with each success his reputation swelled. Joseph was called "a man of intelligence and strength of character." Images of him appeared in popular magazines along with sympathetic stories of the Indians' plight.

The Indians' friendliness to the Montana whites, their refusal to scalp or mutilate the bodies of dead soldiers, and the chiefs' humane treatment of their prisoners all impressed the American public. Many were convinced that the Indians displayed "the highest characteristics recognized by civilized nations," as was written in a Montana paper. And although he did not know it, Chief Joseph was becoming, for some, a hero.

While Howard's men rested, the commanding general of the United States Army, William T. Sherman, came up with a plan for capturing the Indians. Several units were sent to encircle the Indians' position. Almost every route out of the park would be guarded so the Indians would be trapped. Howard's job would be to push the Indians through the park toward one of the waiting armies.

Howard set out again with his men on August 27, 1877, crossing the mountains and entering the park after the Indians. Military spokesmen, confident that the Indians had been caught in a foolproof trap, quickly spread the word that the Nez Perce war would soon be over.

The Indians, meanwhile, were picking their way through rugged territory toward the Clark's Fork of the Yellowstone River, unaware that a Colonel Samuel D. Sturgis was waiting for them there with six companies of cavalry. But suddenly the Indians changed direction and headed south. The colonel's scouts spotted them along a trail that led to the Shoshone River. Sturgis immediately ordered his men to move down to guard the Shoshone River instead of the Clark's Fork.

But the Nez Perces had no intention of following the Shoshone River out of the park. They had gone south only to throw Howard's scouts off their trail. After following the path for a couple of miles, the Indians walked their horses in circles to blur their trail. Then they headed north again and threaded their way through a narrow canyon and moved out of the park, leaving Howard *and* Sturgis far behind. By the time Sturgis caught up with Howard, the Indians had already started across the plains, 50 miles ahead of the American forces.

The Buffalo Country

The Indians hurried north toward the Musselshell River. Unable to keep up with them with all his supplies and ammunition, Sturgis sent his Crow and Bannock scouts ahead to make sure he didn't lose their trail.

Some of the Nez Perces' bitterest memories of the war would involve these Indian scouts. The Bannocks were ancient enemies of the Nez Perce tribes, and they were ruthless fighters. When they discovered sick or wounded Nez Perce men or women on the trail they immediately killed and scalped them. At the Big Hole battlefield the Bannocks dug up the Indian corpses and scalped them and left the bodies exposed.

"We never scalp our enemies," Joseph said, "but when General Howard came up and joined General Gibbon, their Indian scouts dug up our dead and scalped them. I have been told that General Howard did not order this great shame to be done."

The Nez Perces were also outraged that the Crows were helping the soldiers. Looking Glass had often spoken of his friendship with the Crows. In earlier years, he and other Nez Perce warriors had helped the Crows fight the Sioux Indians. Now the Nez Perces expected their friends to return the favor.

But the Crows wanted Nez Perce horses, so instead of helping the fleeing bands they joined the soldiers' chase.

"Crows!" Yellow Wolf said. "A new tribe fighting Chief Joseph. Many snows the Crows had been our friends. But now...turned enemies. My heart felt just like fire."

Well ahead of Sturgis and his men, for two days the Crows and Bannocks chased the bands and raided their herds. The Nez Perce warriors had to guard the moving camp on every side. Small groups of Crows and Bannocks attacked and retreated and then attacked again wherever the Nez Perce forces seemed weak. They cut down two old men who strayed too far from camp, drove several horses away from the herd, harassed the women as they packed, and killed a warrior before the Nez Perce braves finally drove them away.

The Nez Perces continued north, crossing the Musselshell River on September 17 and hurrying on toward the Missouri River. They had to move quickly. It was clear the soldiers would come after them as long as they stayed in the United States.

But they were getting tired. Each morning the women packed the horses and the families headed out, driving the herds another 20 or 30 miles across the unfamiliar land. Day after day they hurried forward, until the days lost their distinction. The sky brightened and darkened, and the earth rose under their feet, widening into mountains shaggy with forest growth, dropping into rocky canyons, or flattening into vast stretches of empty prairie. For more than three months they had been driving the weary horses ahead, and burying their dead along the trail. On and on they went, trying to cover as many miles as they could before evening caught them, pushing themselves until they could think of nothing but rest. But they couldn't stop for rest. They had to keep moving, keep their eyes on the horizon, keep looking out for soldiers, keep reassuring one another that the journey would come to an end before the last of them had died.

Their fear drove them on. It seemed the land was full of enemies. The people of Montana had turned against them, and then their "friends" the Crows had joined the soldiers' chase. How could they be sure another enemy would not appear? Poker Joe told them Sitting Bull would welcome them once they made it to the Canadian border. But they had to get there as quickly as possible.

The effort was wearing them out. More and more of the sick and elderly fell behind. Some of the horses died from exhaustion, others were lamed and had to be abandoned on the trail. Winter was coming, they had only a few lodges, and they were running out of food.

Looking Glass had been arguing with Poker Joe for several days about the pace, telling the half-blood he was driving the people too hard. He said the families needed time to rest and hunt or they would never make it to the border. And when Looking Glass complained in council that only a chief should be allowed to lead, Poker Joe finally gave in.

"All right, Looking Glass, you can lead," he said. "I am trying to save the people, doing my best to cross into Canada before the soldiers find us. You can take command, but I think we will be caught and killed."

And so it was decided. None of the other chiefs objected when Looking Glass began to issue orders.

Looking Glass had the people stop early each afternoon for the next few days, assuring the families that they had plenty of time to rest. The soldiers were at least two days away, he said, and wouldn't catch them as long as they kept moving.

The Nez Perces had traveled over 200 miles since leaving Yellowstone Park. Hounded by Sturgis and then chased by his Indian scouts, they had hurried almost directly north. They had crossed the Yellowstone, Musselshell, and Missouri rivers without being caught. Looking Glass was confident they would make it to their goal.

Then they came to the Bear Paws Mountains. Looking Glass brought them to a site where they could see the barren plains beyond. An icy wind whipped across the prairie, where there were hardly any trees. The emptiness seemed to stretch all the way to Canada. The Indians were less than 40 miles from the border.

The people moved down between the hills and found a site where they could rest out of the wind. A few of the men killed some buffalo and brought the fresh meat down to the camp. Looking Glass said the people would do no more traveling that day.

But one of the braves, a man named Wottolen, objected to the early stop. Wottolen had dreamed that soldiers would attack the camp at dawn. Looking Glass laughed at Wottolen's dream. He said Howard and Sturgis were too far behind to threaten the Indians now.

But another force was following the bands, led by a soldier named Nelson Miles. On the plains, some of the Nez Perce hunters had seen Cheyenne warriors in the distance. Since it was not unusual to see other Indians on the plains, the Nez Perce hunters had ignored the Cheyennes and gone on with their work, unaware that these Indians were scouts for another army that waited just out of sight, hidden beyond the earth's edge.

Bear Paws

The soldiers appeared the next morning, just as Wottolen had dreamed it, 400 men on horseback, stampeding the buffalo on the plains and swarming down among the hills. Children playing with sticks and mud balls along the creek looked up to see Cheyenne warriors on the bluffs above the camp, their war bonnets bending in the wind.

The earth rumbled like thunder, and Chief Joseph ran out of his lodge. "Horses! Horses!" he shouted. "Save the horses!" He rushed to catch the animals before they panicked and fled.

The rumbling grew louder and soldiers topped the hills above the camp, their rifles cocked. "Then the crack of guns filled the air," a Nez Perce named Shot In Head recalled. "Everybody was outside, running here, there, everywhere."

At one end of the camp a group of warriors rushed up the hill to meet the soldiers, and the Indians' gunfire cut the first men down and drove the others back in fear. But another line of soldiers charged into the Indians' horse herd, where families were scrambling for mounts. The soldiers fired, and the horses bucked and shied in the noise. Women, children, young and old struggled to hold onto their mounts. Joseph and a few of the warriors fought to keep the horses under control, but the

Bear Paw Mountain battlefield. (Historical Photograph Collections, Washington State University Libraries, c. 1935, Negative No. 70-0241, Photographer: Emil Kopac.)

soldiers drove hundreds of animals away. The families were forced to run and hide in ditches along the creek.

"My little daughter, 12 years of age, was with me," Joseph recalled. "I gave her a rope and told her to catch a horse and join the others who were cut off from the camp."

Then Joseph grabbed a horse and looked back toward the south end of the camp, where the fighting was thickest. "I thought of my wife and children...surrounded by soldiers, and I resolved to go to them or die," Joseph said. "With a prayer in my mouth...I dashed unarmed through the line of soldiers. It seemed to me that there were guns on every side, before and behind me. My clothes were cut to pieces and my horse was wounded, but I was not hurt."

Abandoning the horse, Joseph plunged into his lodge.

"Here's your gun," his wife said when she saw him, immediately handing him his rifle. "Fight!"

"The soldiers kept up a continuous fire," Joseph remembered. "Six of my men were killed in one spot near me. Ten or 12 soldiers charged into our camp and got possession of two lodges.... I called my men to drive them back. We fought at close range, not more than 20 steps apart, and drove the soldiers back upon their main line, leaving their dead in our hands."

The battle raged all around the camp, but the warriors stopped the soldiers' advance. Several white officers were killed. One detachment of cavalry lost nearly half its fighting men.

The fighting continued for several hours. Then darkness swallowed the battlefield and the firing slowed. The wind grew colder and a few snowflakes fell. The families needed shelter, so they dug into the earth with whatever tools they had.

"We digged the trenches with camas hooks and butcher knives," an Indian woman later said. "With pans we threw out the dirt." These trenches would provide their only protection from the soldiers' fire. For some, it would not be enough.

The people worked all night, digging several kinds of holes. "Shelter pits for the old, the women, the children," Yellow Wolf said. "Rifle pits for the warriors, the fighters." And graves for the many warriors who'd been killed.

Chief Joseph's brother, Ollokot, was among the dead. He had been shot that morning as he fought the soldiers on a ridge above the camp. Poker Joe had also been killed. Toohoolhoolzote was dead, and several other warriors had also been slain.

"We lost, the first day and night, 18 men and three women," Joseph remembered.

"Everywhere the crying," Yellow Wolf said, "the death wail."

Worst of all, the survivors were trapped. Soldiers surrounded them. Since most of the horses had been driven off, the Indians could not escape. They had only one hope left. In council the chiefs decided to send six men to Canada to find Sitting Bull. Perhaps the Sioux would come help the Indians.

Sneaking through the soldiers' lines late that night, the six men set out for the border. In camp, children were crying from the cold, but the Indians could not build any fires. They felt the cold wetness of snow drenching their hair and clothes. By morning five inches of snow had coated the battlefield with icy whiteness and covered the bodies of the dead.

The sky was also white, and a howling wind swept down between the hills, drowning out almost all the sounds of battle. Bullets rained down and shells burst between the trenches, making ugly craters in the snow. The women and children huddled in their pits, holding buffalo robes over their heads as shields. The people were frightened and losing hope.

"I felt the coming end," Yellow Wolf said. "All for which we had suffered lost!…The war deepened. Grew louder…. Everything was against us. No hope! Only bondage or death!"

That afternoon a white flag went up in the soldiers' camp, and the firing stopped. Then someone shouted across the lines, "Colonel Miles would like to see Chief Joseph!"

The Indians quickly formed a council to discuss the matter. Chief Joseph wanted to go and meet the white commander, but the other chiefs were afraid he would surrender. Joseph assured them that he only wanted to find out what the colonel had to say. Reluctantly, the other chiefs agreed to let him go.

Joseph and Miles first met out in the open, at a spot halfway between the camp and the soldiers' line. After a while Joseph agreed to cross into the military camp and continue the discussion in the colonel's tent.

"I walked on to General Miles' tent.... He said, 'Come, let us sit down by the fire and talk this matter over,'" Joseph said.

But the two men could come to no agreement. Through an interpreter, Miles told Joseph he wanted the Indians to surrender, but Joseph refused. When Joseph got up to leave, Miles had his guards restrain him. Suddenly Joseph had become a prisoner. Miles was violating the flag of truce.

Yellow Wolf had followed the morning's events closely, hopeful that Joseph and Miles would be able to negotiate a peace. "Then there was a trick," Yellow Wolf said. "The white flag was pulled down.... That white flag was a lie!" The Indians were furious.

About this time an officer named Jerome rode into the Indian camp. Lieutenant Jerome thought the Indians were about to surrender, and came across the lines to make sure they didn't hide any of their weapons. But when he wandered into their camp the warriors pulled Jerome off his horse. They dragged him to a shelter pit, making him *their* prisoner.

The chiefs told the warriors not to hurt him. "Treat him right," they said. "He is one of the commanders." They hoped to trade the lieutenant for Joseph.

But the fighting resumed. A wagon train arrived that afternoon for the soldiers, bringing a Napoleon cannon. Colonel Miles immediately began to shell the Indian camp.

At last the white sky faded into evening. Again it snowed heavily, and the Indians worked on their trenches and pits. "Children cried with hunger and cold," an Indian woman said. "Old people suffering in silence. Misery everywhere. Cold and dampness all around."

"I was very anxious about my people," Joseph said, recalling his feelings as he waited through the night. "I knew that we were near Sitting Bull's camp in King George's Land [Canada], and I thought maybe the Nez Perces who had escaped would return with assistance. No great damage was done to either party during the night."

The next day the gunfire slowed. Colonel Miles still hoped the Indians would surrender, or that Sturgis or Howard would arrive before the Indians got aid. He knew that some of the Nez Perces had escaped. He had sent a detachment of soldiers after them to prevent their reaching the Sioux, but he didn't know how many Indians had crept through his lines in the dark. Now he looked anxiously to the north, afraid that Sitting Bull would appear before more soldiers could arrive.

The Indians also watched for the Sioux, and later that morning a hundred black dots appeared on the horizon — like an army rapidly approaching. Was it Sturgis and his soldiers, hurrying to crush the Indian forces, or a hundred Sioux warriors coming to help them win the war? The soldiers and Indians kept their eyes on the dots until the dots turned into horsemen — No! It was nothing but a herd of buffalo moving across the distant plains, their humped backs spotted with snow.

Finally Miles agreed to exchange Joseph for Jerome. The white flag was hoisted, and both sides brought their prisoner forward. The hostages shook hands, and each returned to his own camp. The flag came down again, and the battle continued.

"It was slowed up fighting," Yellow Wolf said. "Cloudy, snowy, we did not see the sun set. Full darkness coming, the fighting mostly stopped.... All night we remained in those pits. The cold grew stronger. The wind was filled with snow. Only a little sleep....A long night."

"My people were divided about surrendering," Joseph said. "We could have escaped from Bear Paw Mountain if we had left

Nelson Miles.
(Montana Historical
Society, Helena.)

our wounded, old women and children behind. We were un-willing to do this. We have never heard of a wounded Indian recovering while in the hands of white men."

The next day the fighting continued without interruption. The war chiefs would not give up as long as there was hope the Sioux would arrive. They kept looking to the north, but no warriors appeared there.

Chief Joseph wanted it to end. His heart was heavy for his dead brother, and it hurt him to see his people suffering. The children were crying, and the people were hungry, miserable and losing hope. How long could it go on? Would the warriors fight until every one of them had been killed and there were only a few widows and orphans left to fall into the soldiers' hands?

The next morning a cannon shell hit one of the shelter pits. The impact caved in the pit's earth walls, burying the women and children inside. The Indians rushed to the pit, dug the earth and pulled out three women and a boy, still alive. One girl and her grandmother had been killed, and the pit was converted into a grave.

"It was bad that cannon guns should be turned on the shelter pits where were no fighters," Yellow Wolf said. "Only women and children, old and wounded men in those pits. General Miles and his men handling the big gun surely knew no warriors were in that part of camp."

That afternoon General Howard finally arrived. He had come ahead of most of his men, bringing two aides, two Nez Perce scouts, 17 cavalrymen, and Arthur Chapman, the Idaho volunteer who had fired the first shots of the war. The next day the two Nez Perce scouts, named Old George and Captain John, rode into the Indian camp as messengers for Howard and Miles.

The two scouts dressed like white men, and the warriors watched suspiciously as they approached. Some of the Indians called Captain John "Jokias," a name meaning lazy or worthless. Captain John called out to the warriors in a loud voice, "All my brothers, I am glad to see you alive this sun!" A warrior named Chuslum Hihhih stepped forward to shoot Captain John, but another brave grabbed the gun out of his hand.

After a moment Captain John found his voice. "We have traveled a long ways trying to catch you folks," he said jovially. "We are glad to hear you want no more war, do not want to fight. We are all glad. I am glad because all my sons are glad to be alive. Not to go in battle anymore."

"We have come far from home," Old George spoke up, repeating what Captain John had already said. "You now see many soldiers lying down side by side. We see Indians too, lying dead. I am glad today we are shaking hands. We are all not mad. We all think of Chief Joseph and these others as brothers. We see your sons and relations lying dead, but we are glad to shake hands with you today."

"You, my brothers, have your ears open to me," Old George went on. "General Miles and Chief Joseph will make friends and not let each other go today."

The two men spoke like this for a while, reassuring the fighters that Howard and Miles would not punish them, promising them that the two white war-chiefs would let the Indians return to their homes if they surrendered.

When they had finished, Chief Joseph told them to leave, and the chiefs and warriors got together in council. The people were divided. "All feared to trust General Howard and his soldiers," Yellow Wolf said. The Indians remembered the promises made in the wars of the 1850s, when a white commander named Colonel George H. Wright had tricked the Spokans and other fighting Indians into surrendering their weapons. Almost immediately he had many of them hanged.

"Some of us said to Chief Joseph," Yellow Wolf said, "'We are afraid if you go with General Howard he will hang you.'"

But Joseph chose to believe the white commanders, and he wanted the war to end. Looking Glass and White Bird, however, refused to turn themselves over to the whites. "I am older than you," Looking Glass said to Joseph. "I have my experiences with a man of two faces and two tongues. If you surrender you will be sorry; and in your sorrow you will feel rather to be dead, than suffer that deception."

But Joseph had made up his mind. "I could not bear to see my wounded men and women suffer any longer; we had lost enough already," Joseph explained. "General Miles had promised that we might return to our own country with what stock we had left. I thought we could start again. I believed General Miles, or *I never would have surrendered.*"

"Many of our people are out on the hills, naked and freezing," Joseph said to the council. "The women are suffering with cold, the children crying from the chilly dampness of the shelter pits. For myself I do not care. It is for them I am going to surrender."

But Looking Glass would not be moved. "I will never surrender to a deceitful white chief," he said, and with this the council ended. These were Looking Glass' last words at council. A few minutes later he was shot by one of the soldiers' Cheyenne scouts. He was the last Indian to die in the Nez Perce War.

Joseph told his people he was going to surrender, then picked up his rifle and climbed onto his horse. Some of his men walked beside him a while, and he bent over to hear what they said as they climbed the hill above the creek. Howard and Miles and their aides and orderlies waited at a spot below the soldiers' main line. As Joseph drew nearer the whites could see that his face and one of his wrists were scratched by bullets. His clothes were also torn with bullet holes, but he was not wounded.

When they got to the top of the hill the Indians on foot stopped and turned away. One of Howard's lieutenants named C.E.S. Wood described the scene:

> Joseph threw himself off his horse, draped his blanket about him, and carrying his rifle in the hollow of one arm...held himself very erect, and with a quiet pride, not exactly defiance, advanced toward General Howard and held out his rifle in token of submission. General Howard smiled at him, but waved him over to

Colonel Miles, who was standing beside him. Joseph quickly made a slight turn and offered the rifle to Miles, who took it. Then Joseph stepped back a little.

"Tell General Howard I know his heart," Joseph began, speaking to Arthur Chapman, Howard's interpreter. "What he told me before, I have it in my heart. I am tired of fighting. Our chiefs are killed. Looking Glass is dead. Toohoolhoolzote is dead. The old men are all dead."

Joseph paused and looked back toward the battlefield. "It is the young men who say 'Yes' or 'No,'" the chief continued, remembering his brother, Ollokot. "He who led the young men is dead," he said, his voice suddenly weak. "It is cold, and we have no blankets. The little children are freezing to death. My people, some of them, have run away to the hills and have no blankets, no food. No one knows where they are — perhaps freezing to death. I want to have time to look for my children and see how many of them I can find. Maybe I shall find them among the dead. Hear me, my chiefs! I am tired. My heart is sick and sad....

"From where the sun now stands, I will fight no more forever."

With that Joseph pulled his blanket up over his head, waiting for whatever would come next.

After the End

When Joseph surrendered it seemed that nothing more could be lost. One hundred twenty Indians had died in the war, almost half of them women and children. Ollokot had been killed, as had most of the other chiefs. Another 233 Nez Perces had slipped away from the Bear Paws camp and disappeared, some of them leaving after the surrender. These people ran for the Canadian border, hoping to make that goal at last.

Some of the runaways were captured by soldiers and returned to camp, and some were killed by hostile Indians. The rest vanished. Chief Joseph's daughter was among those who disappeared. After the surrender Joseph sent his nephew, Yellow Wolf, to find her. But when neither Yellow Wolf nor the girl returned, Joseph was forced to leave without them.

Three days after the surrender the Indian prisoners marched out of Bear Paws under guard. They were told they were going to a place called Fort Keogh for the winter and that, in the spring, the soldiers would take them back to their homes.

But two weeks later, the Indians were moved again. The soldiers put the sick and elderly on flatboats and floated them down the Yellowstone River. The rest were taken by land to a more distant place. It made no sense. They were traveling east,

Chief Joseph. (Smithsonian Institution Photo No. 43201-A.)

not west toward their homeland. When they reached the Missouri River, they learned they were headed to North Dakota, and they grew afraid. Perhaps the soldiers meant to hang them after all, just as White Bird and Looking Glass had warned.

But when their wagon train pulled into Bismarck, North Dakota, the Indians were greeted by a cheering crowd. The streets were packed with people, all smiling and waving and shaking the prisoners' hands. A strange rhythmic noise pounded and blasted as they approached: a band was serenading them. All of Bismarck had come out to welcome Joseph. They had even prepared a banquet for him. And although he could not read it, his invitation had been printed in the Bismarck newspaper. It read:

> To Joseph, Head Chief of the Nez Perces.
> Sir:
> Desiring to show you our kind feelings and the admiration we have for your bravery and humanity, as exhibited in your recent conflict with the forces of the United States, we most cordially invite you to dine with us at the Sheridan House in this city. The dinner to be given at 1 1/2 p.m. today.

Instead of a hanging, Joseph was given a banquet. To the people of Bismarck, he was a hero. But the party did not cheer the Indian captives at all. They were beginning to realize that the soldiers were taking them to the Indian Territory, where thousands of other Indians had died. "When will the white man learn to tell the truth?" Chief Joseph wanted to know.

The next day the Nez Perces were put on a train bound for Kansas. Some of them had heard about this "great iron horse that had the speed of a hundred ponies that lived on wood and water," but none of them expected the frightful noise and speed and power of this machine. It was a monster that swallowed up iron rails in front and spit them out behind. For four days the Nez Perces rode in its belly as it thundered down the rails. The land raced by, the hillsides drifted backwards and disappeared, and the countryside flattened out. The Indians had been torn from the earth and shot over the land like a cannonball. When the train stopped, it was impossible to tell how far they'd gone.

The train stopped frequently at water tanks along the way, and at each stop the people piled out of the crowded cars to try and quench their terrible thirst. The air was heavy and dry in this new country, and they could not get enough to drink.

At one of these water stops the train pulled out again without Joseph. The chief watched helplessly as the train moved away, chugging off in a bundle of steam. There was nothing to do but chase the strange machine that wound into the distance. Eventually the train grew big again, as it backed slowly over the rails, returning for him. Joseph hurried anxiously along the tracks to meet the iron horse.

The Indians were finally dumped in a polluted swamp called Fort Leavenworth, Kansas. Colonel Miles had protested this move to his superiors, but the military officials had chosen to deposit the Nez Perces here for the winter, until a permanent home could be found for them. The radical change of climate would prove disastrous for the Indians.

"At Leavenworth we were placed on a low river bottom," Joseph said, "with no water except river-water to drink and cook with. We had always lived in a healthy country, where the mountains were high and the water was cold and clear. Many of my people sickened and died, and we buried them in this strange land. I cannot tell how much my heart suffered for my people while at Leavenworth."

The people were dying from malaria, a disease spread by the mosquitoes that thrived in the hot dampness of the lowlands. The Indians had never been exposed to malaria before, and their bodies offered little resistance to the sickness that invaded their blood.

"It was simply horrible," one observer reported, after visiting the Indian camp in the spring of 1878. It seemed that General Sherman of the War Department had chosen the site "for the express purpose of putting an end to Chief Joseph and his band." By July at least 21 people had died from the disease, and yet the whites seemed unconcerned.

"The Great Spirit Chief who rules above seemed to be looking some other way," Joseph said, "and did not see what was being done to my people."

Seven months earlier Joseph and some of the other Indians had sent a petition to the government requesting permission to return west, or at least to a healthier site. General Sherman denied their request, scrawling the word "DISAPPROVED" across the petition and warning the officials at Leavenworth not to send him such correspondence again. General Sherman regarded the Indians as pests and recommended that they all be exterminated. "The more we kill this year," he once observed, "the less will have to be killed the next war, for the more I see of these Indians, the more convinced I am that they all have to be killed or be maintained as a species of paupers."

But Joseph could not witness his people's terrible suffering in the exile camps without trying to change it. He believed the Nez Perce people had been wronged, and he would not be silent about it.

With the heat of summer the Indians' suffering grew worse. The Indian Bureau decided to move the Nez Perces to Baxter Springs, Kansas, a site just as unhealthy as Fort Leavenworth.

"During the hot days...we received notice that we were to be moved farther away from our own country," Joseph recalled. "We were not asked if we were willing to go. We were ordered to get into the railroad cars. Three of my people died on the way to Baxter Springs. It was worse to die there than to die fighting in the mountains."

There was no shelter for the Indians at their new camp site, and no medicine for those who got the "shaking sickness." By October another 47 had died from the disease.

A year had passed since the surrender, and the people were no better off. Now they waged a different war against disease and depression, and they were losing. Death settled in among them at the place they called Eeikish Pah (The Hot Place), touching them all with fevers and chills. Their white caretakers did not give them any quinine, the only medicine for malaria.

But not all whites were indifferent to the Indians' suffering. Joseph's pleas had reached a few officials in Washington, and that October the Commissioner of Indian Affairs visited the Nez Perce camp. Seeing the dreadful conditions, Commissioner Hayt agreed to let the Indians choose a healthier site in the Indian Territory. Joseph still argued for the right to return west, but agreed to move to an Indian reserve in northern Oklahoma.

The chief had several other visitors at this time. A congressional investigating committee arrived, led by Lafayette Grover, the former governor of Oregon who had once written to President Grant protesting the Wallowa reservation, and who now claimed to be Joseph's friend. Military men, congressmen and journalists appeared, each of them witnessing the misery of the exiled Indians firsthand, and each of them assuring Joseph they would do what they could to help him. But only one man, Indian Inspector General John O'Neill, actually lived up to his word.

Convinced that Joseph could speak most eloquently for himself, O'Neill arranged a trip to Washington, D.C., for a meeting with President Rutherford B. Hayes.

Going to Washington

And so it was decided. Joseph would go to see the president. He set out in January, leaving his people on the Kansas reserve, taking only an Indian named Yellow Bull, and Arthur Chapman, who'd been hired as an interpreter.

As he stared out of his train window Joseph wondered what the president would be like. Would he welcome the Indians? Would he shake their hands and listen to all they said? Would he be moved by their story, surprised and ashamed for the harm his country had done to their people?

For years the white commissioners and agents had told the Indians that the president had ordered this or that to be done. The president had given them their treaties. The president had agreed to let Joseph's people stay in the Wallowa, and then the president had changed his mind. The president had ordered Howard to push the Indians off their lands. The president had decided to break Colonel Miles' word, sending the Indians to a hot land where it was obvious they would sicken and die.

But sometimes it wasn't the president. Sometimes it was just "Washington." Colonel Miles had told Joseph he'd had orders from Washington, from a chief above him — not from the president. General Howard and agent Monteith had also

114

said *Washington*. They said they had orders, instructions from Washington. So what was Washington?

"You are always talking about *Washington*," Toohoolhoolzote had said to General Howard in the last council before the war. "I would like to know who Washington is? Is he a chief or a common man, or a house or a place? Every time you have a council you speak of Washington. Leave Mr. Washington ...if he is a man, alone. He has no sense. He does not know anything about our country. He never was here."

Joseph was also confused. What was this American government, this place where so many chiefs contradicted one another and even themselves at times? How did it work? Joseph hoped that on this trip he would find the answers to these questions.

As he looked out of his train window, it seemed as though he was speeding into the future. The countryside changed rapidly. Isolated cabins turned into farms and settlements, houses grew taller, forests thinned and retreated, and the color bled out of the sky. Finally the train entered a huge wooden cage, a bridge over a wide river that had what sounded like an Indian name: the Potomac. Across that river was Washington.

The city was strange to Joseph. The houses were tall and skinny like trees in a forest, and planted as close together. The people all seemed to be dressed in their finest clothes, the women in wide skirts that floated above the ground, hiding their feet, and large bonnets that looked like war shields strapped to their heads. The men wore spotless hats and high collars and shiny hard shoes. Fine horse-drawn wagons trundled down the streets, day and night. No one seemed to sleep in this bustling city. Perhaps they were confused by the fact that it never got dark, since the streets were lined with tall black poles with fires on top that burned without wood and flickered but never went out. More than ever Joseph felt he was in an alien land. Everywhere he went the people stopped and stared at him, making him feel anxious and lonely for home.

Joseph and his companions would have to wait several days before they could see the president. In the meantime Joseph had been invited to speak at a gathering of people interested in his story: congressmen and cabinet members who'd read about him during the war, or who'd voted to ratify one treaty or another. These men wanted to see the Indian who had been called the Napoleon of his people. Most of them knew very little about the Nez Perce Indians, but they had heard plenty about Joseph's kindness and intelligence. Joseph understood he would be speaking to a large group of "law chiefs," men who had some power in Washington.

When it was time for the council to begin he and Yellow Bull and Arthur Chapman were taken to a large government building and led onto a platform in a wide hall that was already crowded with people. Joseph and his companions found their places in chairs alongside several other people, including another Indian chief, a Ute called Little Red.

Joseph gazed out across the collection of white faces looking up at him in expectation. The crowd was quiet. They seemed to be waiting eagerly, so Joseph introduced himself, explaining that he was chief of the Wellamotkin band of Nez Perces, a position he had inherited from his father. Then he told how his father had died. "He left a good name on the earth," Joseph said. "He advised me well for my people."

Joseph spoke about how the first white men appeared on Indian lands when his father was just a child. He described the missionary "who talked spirit law," and told how white settlers swarmed over the land after the missionaries arrived.

116

He described the early councils, the taunts and threats the white settlers made against his people, and the murders and outrages the Indians had suffered without retaliation.

And then Joseph described how the whites had forced the Indians off their lands.

"In the treaty councils the commissioners have claimed that our country had been sold to the Government," Joseph said. "Suppose a white man should come to me and say, 'Joseph, I like your horses, and I want to buy them.' I say to him, 'No, my horses suit me, I will not sell them.' Then he goes to my neighbor, and says to him: 'Joseph has some good horses. I want to buy them, but he refuses to sell.' My neighbor answers, 'Pay me the money, and I will sell you Joseph's horses.' The white man returns to me, and says, 'Joseph, I have bought your horses, and you must let me have them.' If we sold our lands to the Government, this is the way they were bought."

The crowd was with him. From time to time they even applauded. Most of them had never heard this version of the events that led to the war.

Joseph described General Howard at the last council before the war, how Howard had threatened to bring in soldiers, arrested Toohoolhoolzote, and given the Indians an unreasonable deadline for moving to the reservation.

He talked about the war, the slaughter of Indian women and children, the final surrender, and Colonel Miles' promise to send the Indians back home. Then he described the hot land where his people had been taken, and the death and misery that waited for them there. And as he spoke he looked into the eyes of his listeners. Were they truly hearing him? Would this trip to Washington make a difference?

"The Earth Is the Mother of All People"

His story had come to an end, but Joseph wasn't finished. He wanted the people to look forward. What would become of the Indians and the whites? Would they always settle their differences with wars? He wanted a more hopeful future.

"If the white man wants to live in peace with the Indian, he can live in peace," Joseph said. "There need be no trouble. Treat all men alike. Give them all the same law. Give them all an even chance to live and grow. All men were made by the same Great Spirit Chief. They are all brothers. The earth is the mother of all people, and all people should have equal rights upon it."

"I only ask...to be treated as all other men are treated. If I cannot go to my own home, let me have a home in some country where my people will not die so fast. I would like to go to Bitterroot Valley. There my people would be healthy; where they are now they are dying. Three have died since I left my camp to come to Washington."

"When I think of our condition my heart is heavy. I see men of my race treated as outlaws and driven from country to country, or shot down like animals."

118

"I know my race must change. We can not hold our own with the white men as we are. We only ask an even chance to live as other men live. We ask to be recognized as men. We ask that the same law shall work alike on all men."

"Let me be a free man — free to travel, free to stop, free to work, free to trade where I choose, free to choose my own teachers, free to follow the religion of my fathers, free to think and talk and act for myself — and I will obey every law, or submit to the penalty."

"Whenever the white man treats the Indian as they treat each other, then we will have no more wars. We shall all be alike — brothers of one father and one mother, with one sky above us and one country around us, and one government for all. Then the Great Spirit Chief who rules above will smile upon this land, and send rain to wash out the bloody spots made by brothers' hands from the face of the earth....

"Hin-mah-too-yah-lat-kehkt has spoken."

Indian Territory

Good words do not last long unless they amount to something," Joseph had said. "Words do not pay for my dead people. They do not pay for my country.... Good words will not give my people good health and stop them from dying. Good words will not get my people a home where they can live in peace and take care of themselves."

And the audience had applauded and afterwards many had shaken his hand and assured him they would do whatever they could to help.

But nothing had come of it. Joseph had even met with President Hayes, but the discussion had lasted only a few minutes. Nothing could be decided in so little time. No plans were made to give the Nez Perces a better home. Instead they were moved to the Indian Territory in Oklahoma.

Oklahoma was not much better than Kansas. Although the land was a little greener, the people could not adapt to the harsh climate of the low country. There were no high mountain valleys where they could go to escape the heat, no sheltered canyons where they could move to avoid the bitter cold.

The Indians' lodges were so old their canvas coverings began to rot, and the snows and rains of winter leaked through and drenched them and their belongings. Since they had no guns or horses, they could not hunt for themselves, and were dependent on the meager rations the government supplied. In summer the warm water carried strange diseases that made them sick. Almost every other week Joseph buried another member of his band.

The months lengthened into years as Joseph waited for something to be done. Almost every child born in the Indian Territory also died there. One visitor counted a hundred graves of infants and children. Among them was Joseph's youngest daughter, the baby he had struggled so hard to protect during the war. For perhaps the first time in his life, Joseph was overcome with despair.

Each time he had a visitor Joseph complained of the horrible conditions of the camp. He showed his white friends the Indian cemetery, filled with the graves of Nez Perce children.

"You come to see me as you would a man upon his death-bed," Joseph told a group of visitors one year. "The Great Spirit above has left me and my people to their fate. The white men forget us, and death comes almost every day for some of my people. He will come for all of us. A few months more and we will be in the ground. We are a doomed people."

But Joseph's efforts over the years eventually began to have some effect. His courage and sincerity even converted some of his former enemies into friends. In 1881, Nelson Miles, who had forced Joseph's people to surrender, made a personal appeal to President Hayes asking that the Indians be returned to Idaho. C.E.S. Wood, who had served under General Howard, also tried to help Joseph by starting a letter-writing campaign on the Indians' behalf. Christian groups, journalists and activists for

Indian rights publicized Joseph's case, and in time people across the nation were reading and talking about the government's cruel treatment of this "noble Indian" and his followers. Letters and telegrams flowed into Washington until at last the ponderous machinery of American government was set in motion.

Finally, on July 4, 1884, almost seven years after the war, Congress passed an act that gave the Secretary of the Interior the authority to return the Indians to Idaho. A few months later the surviving Nez Perce prisoners were told they would be allowed to return to the Northwest.

But many whites in Idaho still blamed Joseph for the Nez Perce war, and hoped to permanently bar him and his people from the territory. Fearing that these settlers would riot if the chief returned to Idaho, the government decided to transfer half of the Indians to the reservation at Lapwai, and the rest to another reservation, called Colville, in Washington state.

Nespelem

S oon after their arrival at the Colville Reservation, Joseph moved his people to a place called Nespelem, near a creek on a fertile patch of land. Although the countryside of Nespelem was more like the Wallowa than the Indian Territory had been, Joseph still longed for his homeland. He dreamed of one day buying back the country his people had lost, and he began to press the government for a Wallowa reservation. In the meantime he and his people settled at Nespelem.

In some ways their life on the Colville Reservation was good. The people raised horses and cattle, hunted wild game, and caught salmon in the San-poil River. They worshipped as they pleased, without interference from the whites. Most of them ignored the wooden houses the government built for them and used their tepees year-round. In the winter they joined their lodges together and lived in family groups.

But Joseph's people were still prisoners, forced to live by the white man's rules. They were required to ask permission to leave the reservation for any reason. And because they couldn't find enough game and fish to feed themselves within the reservation's borders, they had to rely on the government for a large portion of their food.

Joseph hoped they would not be at Nespelem long, but he adapted to his new home. The summers were pleasantly mild, compared to the terrible heat of Oklahoma. He was grateful that the whites had finally moved his people to a healthier land.

At Nespelem the Indians began to increase their horse and cattle herds. Joseph loved to race horses, and several times each summer his people gathered on a wide plain below the reservation agency to bet on and match their animals. Everyone wore their finest clothes, just as they had before the war.

In late October the tribe split into several groups for the fall hunt, spreading out to comb the countryside for game. Afterward they gathered to divide the meat. Chief Joseph distributed the food to each family according to need. The animal skins were always given to the hunter who'd made the kill.

In 1887, Joseph was invited to move his people to Lapwai. Under a new policy called the Severalty Act, the government had begun dividing the reservation into individual plots of land. The government hoped to persuade the Indians to live like whites. Each Indian man would be given a parcel of land to farm or develop as he pleased. No longer would the Indians share the earth with one another; now they would *own* it.

Joseph refused to accept any land from the government. He had no desire to live like a white man, alone on his own little piece of earth. Nor would he give up on a Wallowa reservation.

"He will have none but the Wallowa Valley, from which he was driven," the allotting agent's assistant wrote, after meeting the chief. "He will remain landless and homeless if he cannot have his own again. It was good to see an unsubjugated Indian. One could not help respecting the man who still stood firmly for his rights, after having fought and suffered and been defeated in the struggle for their maintenance."

Chief Joseph at Nespelem. (Montana Historical Society, Helena.)

Forgiveness

In 1897, Joseph decided to go back to Washington, D.C., this time to complain that white squatters were overrunning the Colville lands. Not even this reservation was protected from the invasions of greedy settlers.

In Washington, Joseph met with President William McKinley and General Miles, both of whom assured him they would look into the problem at Colville. Then Joseph asked that his people be allowed to return to Wallowa. Although Miles supported Joseph, the general could not convince anyone else in the government that such a move would be worthwhile.

While Joseph was in Washington, Miles invited him to go to New York City, where preparations were underway for the dedication of former President Grant's tomb. Miles said there would be a big parade in honor of the dead president, and he invited Joseph to ride with him in a place of honor.

Joseph said he could not afford to make the trip, but when Miles arranged to have his expenses paid, the chief finally agreed.

New York City was like nothing Joseph had ever seen. Enormous buildings shadowed the narrow streets, with windows climbing up to the sky. The sidewalks were jammed with pedestrians — there were too many people. The streets, the buildings, the rooms were all square. Even the sky looked like a ceiling above the walls of the buildings. There was no soil, only flat stone sidewalks and bumpy stone streets. And there were hardly any trees. The air was heavy and thick with smells. It was hard to breathe.

And the city was churning with activity. Thousands of visitors poured in from all parts of the country. Veterans of the Civil War, officers who'd served under Grant, and militias from almost every state came to march in the dedication parade. And strangely, in the midst of this human flood, Chief Joseph ran into a familiar face.

The meeting took place in Madison Square Garden the day before the parade. Joseph and his companions had gone to see a show in the large auditorium, and as they sat near the entrance a stream of newcomers filed past their seats. Suddenly a white-haired man appeared before Joseph, stopping in surprise. Joseph looked up at the one-armed man — it was General Howard!

A reporter had been watching Joseph, and he described the interaction. He said Howard "paused almost in the act of holding out his hand, as if he were in doubt whether his presence might not cause pain to the chief."

Joseph immediately stood up, removed his hat, and took Howard's hand. "I am glad to see you, Joseph," Howard exclaimed, using almost the same words he had used when they first met, "glad to see you!" Then, as in that first encounter, the two found they had little else to say. Howard soon excused himself, moving on to find his seat. A few minutes later General Miles also appeared, and the greeting and handshake were repeated.

As Joseph was leaving the auditorium a reporter asked him if he was going to ride in the parade. The slightly overweight chief laughed and said they might not be able to find a horse that could carry him.

But the next day Joseph appeared on horseback at the start of the parade. Above him a huge American flag flapped in the belfry of a church. After a long wait the procession finally began. With a serious expression on his face, and apparently without misgivings, Chief Joseph marched up Madison Avenue with the two men who had defeated him in war, in a parade that honored the president who had stolen from him his last hope for a reservation on his own land.

Wallowa

In August 1899, Joseph visited the Wallowa for the first time since the war. In the 22 years of his absence, the land of winding waters had completely changed. What had once been open range was now crisscrossed with the white man's fences. Grain and hay fields filled in the spaces between the network of property lines. Neat rows of trees had sprung up where Joseph remembered only grasslands, and prim wood-sided houses had replaced the settlers' rough log cabins.

Four little towns now hugged the banks of the Wallowa River, and the icy waters now flowed into irrigation ditches and canals that fed the farmers' fields.

Joseph visited an old friend, a settler named A.C. Smith, and together they traveled across the Wallowa country. Smith took the chief to a public meeting, and Joseph spoke of his desire to buy some land for his people, but the settlers told him no one would sell any land for an Indian reservation.

A few months later the Indian inspector general, James McLaughlin, visited Joseph at Nespelem. The Indian Bureau had instructed McLaughlin to look into Joseph's request.

In the summer of 1900, McLaughlin and Joseph went back to the Wallowa Valley. While they were there, McLaughlin took

Joseph to look for his father's grave. As they approached the burial site, Joseph realized that it lay on a farmer's land. Long rows of freshly plowed earth stretched as far as he could see. For a moment Joseph feared that his father's grave had been destroyed. But the farmer, a stranger to Joseph, had built a protective fence around it. When Joseph saw it his eyes filled with tears. This tiny plot was all that remained of the great country his father had left him.

After they left the grave, McLaughlin took Joseph to Wallowa Lake. Joseph's friend, A.C. Smith, and several settlers from the area met them there. The settlers told Joseph and the inspector they would never let the Indians return.

Chief Joseph went back to Nespelem to live out the last years of his life. He never gave up his dream of a Wallowa reservation, and even made a third trip to Washington to meet another president, Theodore Roosevelt. General Miles always backed Joseph's claims, but his support was not enough. To the end of his days Joseph insisted that the Wallowa still belonged to his people.

Chief Joseph died September 21, 1904, at his Nespelem camp. On that day he suddenly collapsed while sitting before his tepee fire. The doctor at the agency announced that the chief had died of a broken heart.

When Joseph's wives discovered his body they sent up a wailing cry. The people rushed in from nearby lodges and, with tears and groans, prepared his body for burial.

The people dressed Joseph in his finest clothes, with an enormous headdress on his head. They painted his face and laid him on a litter, and a shaman spoke over his body. For three days the people came to look at him and grieve. Joseph's widows cut their hair short. They could not remarry until their hair grew back to their shoulder blades.

Joseph's lodge was destroyed, and his horses' tails were bobbed. For two years after the burial ceremony, no one would be allowed to ride these animals.

When three days had passed the people moved Joseph's body to a burial site. The Indians spoke out loud of their chief's great deeds, and they wailed and sobbed as his body was put in a wooden coffin and buried beneath a mound of stones.

His family raised a new lodge, and the shaman brought in his sacred pipe. The wise man blew smoke to the four winds, asking them to carry Joseph's spirit back to the spirit land.

Nez Perces on parade. (Special Collections Division, University of Washington Libraries, Negative No. NA 947, Photographer: Latham.)

Notes

Most of this book is structured around Chief Joseph's own account of his life. Although the text of the speech Joseph delivered in Washington, D.C., was never written down, Joseph repeated it soon afterwards for the April 1879 issue of *North American Review*. The translation of Joseph's words was edited heavily for that publication, but the power of his ideas and language comes through nonetheless. Most of the quotes from Chief Joseph are taken from this source.

Another primary source for this book was *The Nez Perce Indians and the Opening of the Northwest,* by Alvin M. Josephy, Jr. In his book, Josephy traces Nez Perce history and culture back to its earliest roots and describes in great detail the settlement of Nez Perce territory by white trappers, missionaries, farmers and ranchers. Josephy also analyzed hundreds of accounts and documents relating to the Nez Perce councils, treaties, the Nez Perce-American War, and the years following the war when the tribe was permanently divided.

The dialogue and descriptions of action during the council meetings were based largely on the Josephy book, but a few quotes were drawn from other sources, primarily Oliver Otis Howard's *Nez Perce Joseph* and Chester A. Fee's biography, *Chief Joseph.*

The chapters describing the war, including quotes from Indians other than Joseph, were based on two books by Lucullus McWhorter: *Hear Me, My Chiefs!* and *Yellow Wolf.* Mark Brown's *The Flight of the Nez Perce* and Merrill D. Beal's *"I Will Fight No More Forever"* were also useful.

Passages describing Joseph's last years were based on the Fee biography, which includes a first-person account from a young man who lived for several months with Chief Joseph in his home in Nespelem, Washington. Also valuable was *With One Sky Above Us,* by Mick Gidley.

For all other sources, see the bibliography.

Bibliography

Beal, Merrill D., *"I Will Fight No More Forever,"* Seattle: University of Washington Press, 1963.

Bond, Fred G., *Flatboating on the Yellowstone*, New York: American Library Association, 1925.

Brown, Mark H., *The Flight of the Nez Perce*, New York: G.P. Putnam's Sons, 1967.

Chief Joseph, "An Indian's View of Indian Affairs," *North American Review*, 128 (April 1879), 412–33.

Fee, Chester A., *Chief Joseph*, New York: Wilson-Erickson, 1936.

Gay, Jane E., *With the Nez Perces*, Lincoln, Nebraska: University of Nebraska Press, 1981.

Gibbon, John, "The Battle of the Big Hole," *Harper's Weekly*, XXXIX (Dec. 21 and 28, 1895), 1215–6 and 1235–6.

Gidley, Mick, *With One Sky Above Us*, Seattle: University of Washington Press, 1979.

Haines, Francis, *The Nez Perces*, Norman, Oklahoma: University of Oklahoma Press, 1955.

Howard, Oliver Otis, *Nez Perce Joseph*, Boston: Lee and Shepard, 1881.

Josephy, Alvin M. Jr., *The Nez Perce Indians and the Opening of the Northwest*, New Haven: Yale University Press, 1965.

McBeth, Kate C., *The Nez Perces Since Lewis and Clarke*, New York: Fleming H. Revell Co., 1908.

McWhorter, Lucullus V., *Hear Me, My Chiefs!* Caldwell, Idaho: Caxton Printers, 1958.

—, *Yellow Wolf*, Caldwell, Idaho: Caxton Printers, 1991.

Chronology

1805   Lewis and Clark visit Nez Perce territory.

1836   The missionaries Henry and Eliza Spalding settle at Lapwai.

1840   Hin-mah-too-yah-lat-kekht (the future Chief Joseph) is born.

1855   Joseph's father, Tuekakas, and the other Nez Perce chiefs sign the Walla Walla Treaty (ratified 1859).

1860   Prospectors discover gold in Nez Perce territory.

1863   Tuekakas and a few other chiefs walk out of a treaty council. The remaining chiefs sign a treaty selling the lands of the absent chiefs.

1871   Tuekakas dies. The first white settlers move into the Wallowa country.

1873   President Ulysses S. Grant signs an executive order for a Wallowa reservation.

1875   President Grant rescinds the order for a Wallowa reservation.

1876   Wilhautyah, a member of Joseph's band, is murdered by two white settlers in the Wallowa. Chief Joseph meets with General Howard and his treaty commission at the mission church at Lapwai. Joseph refuses to give up his land.

1877   *6 January.* The agent, John Monteith, orders Joseph to move his people to the Lapwai reservation. Joseph refuses.

        1 April. Ollokot meets with Lieutenant William H. Boyle at the Umatilla Reservation.

        20 April. Ollokot meets with General Howard at Walla Walla to discuss possible solutions to the conflict over the Wallowa. Howard refuses to negotiate.

1877   *3–7 May.* Last council between Howard and the Nez Perces. Howard arrests the Indians' spokesman, a chief named Toohoolhoolzote, and threatens to send him to the Indian Territory in Oklahoma. Joseph and the other chiefs agree to move to Lapwai Reservation.

14–15 June. Young Nez Perce warriors raid white settlements, killing and wounding several whites. Chief Joseph decides to stay with warring bands. Howard sends troops after fleeing Nez Perces.

17 June. Battle of White Bird Canyon.

1–8 July. Nez Perces outmaneuver General Howard and leave his forces stranded on the west bank of the Salmon River.

1 July. Soldiers attack Looking Glass' peaceful village. Looking Glass decides to join the war.

3–8 July. Nez Perce warriors slaughter a detachment of cavalry, attack the soldiers' encampment at Cottonwood, and flee to the South Fork of the Clearwater River.

11–12 July. Battle of the Clearwater.

16–27 July. Nez Perces cross the Bitterroot Mountains on the Lolo Trail.

28 July. Indians get around a military blockade at the end of the Lolo Trail.

9 August. Battle of the Big Hole.

20 August. Indians raid Howard's camp at the Camas Meadows.

23 August–6 September. Indians cross Yellowstone National Park.

8–29 September. Colonel Sturgis fails to block the Indians' exit from Yellowstone National Park. Nez Perces move north toward Canada, but the soldiers follow.

1877	*30 September–5 October.* Battle of the Bear Paws.
	5 October. Chief Joseph surrenders.
	27 November. Joseph's people are settled at Fort Leavenworth, Kansas.
1878	Joseph's people transferred to the Quawpaw Indian Reserve in Kansas.
1879	Joseph visits Washington, D.C., meets with President Rutherford B. Hayes, and makes speech to lawmakers.
1885	Joseph's people transferred to the Colville Reservation in Nespelem, Washington.
1897	Joseph travels to Washington, D.C., and New York City, meets with President William McKinley, and rides in the parade at the dedication of Grant's tomb.
1899	Joseph visits the Wallowa.
1900	Joseph visits the Wallowa again. Settlers refuse to allow the Indians to return.
1903	Joseph travels to Washington, D.C., again and meets with President Theodore Roosevelt.
1904	Chief Joseph dies in exile on the Colville Reservation.

Index